THE NUTRIBULLET RECIPE BOOK

Healthy Smoothies And More Diabetic-Friendly, Cardiac-Friendly, Cholesterol-Lowering Recipes And Many More!

WINIFRED B. SILVA

Copyright © 2024 By WINIFRED B. SILVA. All rights reserved worldwide.

No part of this book may be reproduced or transmitted in any form or by any means, electronic or mechanical, including photocopying, recording, or by any information storage and retrieval system, without written permission from the publisher, except for the inclusion of brief quotations in a review.

Warning Disclaimer:

The purpose of this book is to educate and entertain. The author or publisher does not guarantee that anyone following the techniques, suggestions, tips, ideas, or strategies will become successful. The author and publisher shall have neither liability nor responsibility to anyone concerning any loss or damage caused, or alleged to be caused, directly or indirectly, by the information contained in this book.

This copyright notice and disclaimer apply to the entirety of the book and its contents, whether in print or electronic form and extend to all future editions or revisions of the book. Unauthorized use or reproduction of this book or its contents is strictly prohibited and may result in legal action.

TABLE OF CONTENTS

Introduction 7

    My Nutribullet Journey 7

    Understanding Your Nutribullet .. 9

    Common Issues and Solutions ... 13

CHAPTER 1: RADIANT SKIN SMOOTHIES 15

    Glowing Green Goddess 15

    Berry Collagen Booster 15

    Cucumber Mint Refresher 16

    Carrot Ginger Glow 16

    Avocado Spinach Hydrator 17

    Pomegranate Antioxidant Blast . 17

    Kiwi Vitamin C Kick 18

    Papaya Enzyme Elixir 18

    Aloe Vera Skin Soother 19

    Beetroot Beauty Blend 19

    Mango Turmeric Radiance 20

    Blueberry Acai Skin Shield 21

    Coconut Water Complexion Clearer 22

CHAPTER 2: ANTIAGING ELIXIRS 23

    Berry AgeDefying Blend 23

    Green Tea Antioxidant Smoothie 23

    Cacao Nib Youth Booster 24

    Omega3 Rich Flaxseed Shake ... 24

    Spirulina Superfood Elixir 25

    Pomegranate Seed Rejuvenator 25

    Kale and Almond AntiWrinkle Blend 26

    Goji Berry Longevity Tonic 26

    Avocado EBooster Smoothie 27

    CollagenSupporting Citrus Blend 27

    ResveratrolRich Red Grape Smoothie 28

    Matcha Green Tea Energy Lift ... 29

Açai Berry AgeReversal Blend .. 30

CHAPTER 3: DETOX AND CLEANSE SMOOTHIES 31

Green Detox Dream 31

Lemon Ginger Flush 31

Activated Charcoal Cleanse 32

Beet and Berry Liver Support ... 32

Cilantro Chelation Blend 33

Dandelion Greens Detoxifier 33

Watermelon Flush 34

Pineapple Enzyme Cleanser 34

Chlorella ClearOut 35

Cranberry Kidney Cleanse 35

Apple Cider Vinegar Detox 36

Turmeric Golden Milk Detoxifier 37

Parsley and Celery Juice Blend 38

CHAPTER 4: WEIGHT LOSS WONDERS 39

Green Metabolism Booster 39

Berry Protein Punch 39

Cinnamon Roll Protein Shake ... 40

Spinach and Pear Slimmer 40

Chia Seed Filling Smoothie 41

Grapefruit Fat Burner 41

Chocolate PB2 Protein Shake 42

Cayenne KickStart Blend 42

Matcha Green Tea Fat Burner 43

Celery and Apple Flat Belly Smoother 43

Pineapple Coconut Metabolism Booster 44

Raspberry Ketone Kicker 45

Cucumber Mint Hydration Helper 46

CHAPTER 5: HEART HEALTH HEROES 47

Oatmeal Berry Heart Helper 47

Spinach Avocado Cholesterol Buster 47

Beet and Pomegranate Pressure REDUCER 48

Omega3 Rich Flax and Chia Blend 48

Green Tea and Berries Artery Cleaner 49

Banana Walnut Potassium Booster 49

Kale and Pineapple Inflammation Fighter 50

Cocoa and Almond Heart Protector 50

Tomato Lycopene Heart Shield .. 51

Watermelon Citrulline Cardio Booster 51

Grape and Resveratrol Heart Tonic 52

Ginger Turmeric Circulation Enhancer 52

Blueberry Oat Fiber Booster 53

Chapter 6: Energy Boosters 53

Green Tea Energiser 54

Beetroot PreWorkout Booster .. 54

Banana Oat Energy Blast 55

Maca Root PowerUp 55

Ginseng Ginger Zing 56

Coconut Water Electrolyte Replenisher 56

Cacao Nib Energy Bites Smoothie 57

Spirulina Superfood Energiser .. 57

Matcha Green Tea Focuser 58

Chia Seed Sustainer 59

BVitamin Boost Blend 59

Guarana Berry Energy Kick 60

CHAPTER 7: SUPERFOOD SENSATIONS 61

Acai Berry Bowl Blend 61

Goji Berry Antioxidant Blast 61

Spirulina Green Goddess 62

Maca Root Hormone Balancer ... 62

Cacao Nib Mood Lifter 63

Chia Seed Omega Booster 63

Hemp Protein PowerUp 64

Moringa Leaf NutrientPacked Smoothie 64

Turmeric Golden Milk Blend 65

Wheatgrass Shot Smoother 65

Matcha Green Tea Antioxidant Elixir 66

Chlorella Cleanse and Energies 67

Bee Pollen Immunity Booster 68

CHAPTER 8: SEASONAL SMOOTHIE SPECIALTIES 69

Summer Berry Blast 69

Autumn Pumpkin Spice Smoothie 69

Winter Citrus Immune Booster . 70

Spring Greens Renewal Blend ... 70

Watermelon Cooler 71

Apple Pie Smoothie 71

Cranberry Orange Winter Tonic 72

Asparagus and Pea Spring Cleanse 72

Peach Melba Summer Slimmer .. 73

Cinnamon Persimmon Fall Warmer 73

Gingerbread Cookie Protein Shake 74

Strawberry Rhubarb Spring Tonic 75

Fig and Honey Autumn Blend 76

CHAPTER 9: KID-FRIENDLY SMOOTHIES 77

Banana Split Smoothie 77

Hidden Veggie Berry Blast 77

Green Monster Shake 78

Peanut Butter and Jelly Smoothie 78

Chocolate Chip Cookie Dough Shake 79

Rainbow Fruit Smoothie 79

Creamsicle Dream 80

Apple Pie A La Mode Smoothie .. 80

Watermelon Slushie 81

nutrient-packed

Tropical Coconut Pineapple Smoothie 82

Purple Power Smoothie 83

Nutella Banana Shake 84

CHAPTER 10: PROTEIN PACKED POSTWORKOUT SMOOTHIES 85

Chocolate Banana Protein Shake 85

Vanilla Almond Muscle Builder .. 85

Berry Blast Recovery Smoothie 86

Green Protein Machine 86

Peanut Butter Cup Protein Shake 87

Tropical Coconut Protein Smoothie 87

Cinnamon Roll Protein Blast 88

Coffee Protein WakeUp Call 88

Cherry Vanilla Muscle Mender ... 89

Blueberry Muffin Protein Shake 89

Key Lime Pie Protein Smoothie . 90

Carrot Cake Protein Shake 90

Strawberry Cheesecake Protein Blast 91

MEAL PLANNING WITH YOUR NUTRIBULLET 92

Measurement Conversions 97

CONCLUSION 103

INTRODUCTION

MY NUTRIBULLET JOURNEY

When I first laid eyes on a Nutribullet in a friend's kitchen, I had no idea how this compact gadget would revolutionise my approach to nutrition and transform my life. As someone who'd always struggled with incorporating enough fruits and vegetables into my diet, the Nutribullet seemed like a potential game-changer. I remember my first attempt at making a smoothie. It was a disaster, to say the least! I'd thrown in a bunch of kale, a whole apple (core and all), and some water. The result was a chunky, bitter concoction that I could barely swallow. But I was determined to crack the code.

Over the next few weeks, I experimented relentlessly. I learned that a balance of fruits and vegetables was key, that liquid ratios mattered, and that ingredients like bananas and avocados could add a creamy texture. Gradually, my smoothies improved, and I found myself looking forward to my daily blends. As I delved deeper into the world of Nutribullet recipes, I discovered it wasn't just about smoothies. I started making homemade nut butter, creamy soups, and even pancake batter. The Nutribullet became my go-to kitchen appliance, saving me time and helping me pack more nutrients into every meal.

The changes in my health were noticeable. My energy levels soared, my skin cleared up, and those stubborn extra pounds started to melt away. Friends and family began to comment on my "glow", and I found myself sharing Nutribullet tips and recipes with anyone who'd listen. This journey wasn't without its hiccups. There were times when I overblended and ended up with frothy messes, or when I added too much of a potent ingredient like ginger or turmeric. But each mistake was a lesson, helping me refine my techniques and expand my recipe repertoire.

As my expertise grew, so did my passion for sharing this knowledge. I started hosting "smoothie parties" for friends, experimented with seasonal ingredients, and even incorporated Nutribullet creations into my holiday menus. What began as a simple attempt to eat healthier had blossomed into a full-fledged lifestyle change. Now, years into my Nutribullet journey, I can confidently say that this little machine has been a catalyst for positive change in my life. It's not just about the physical health benefits – though those are significant – it's about the joy of creation, the satisfaction of nourishing my body, and the pleasure of sharing healthy, delicious concoctions with loved ones.

Through trial and error, research, and a whole lot of blending, I've amassed a wealth of knowledge and recipes that I'm thrilled to share with you in this book.

Whether you're a complete novice or looking to expand your Nutribullet repertoire, I hope my journey inspires you to embark on your adventure in nutrition and wellness.

HOW THIS BOOK WILL TRANSFORM YOUR HEALTH AND LIFESTYLE

Welcome to your comprehensive guide to mastering the Nutribullet and revolutionising your approach to nutrition. This book isn't just a collection of recipes; it's a roadmap to a healthier, more vibrant you. Let me walk you through how this book will become your trusted companion on your journey to better health and a more balanced lifestyle. Firstly, we'll start with the basics. If you're new to the Nutribullet, don't worry – I've got you covered. We'll go through everything from setting up your machine to understanding its different functions. You'll learn about the importance of layering ingredients, the right liquid-to-solid ratios, and how to achieve that perfect consistency every time.

But we won't stop at the mechanics. This book dives deep into the nutritional science behind Nutribullet blending. You'll discover how blending can increase nutrient absorption, why certain food combinations can boost your health, and how to tailor your smoothies to your specific health goals. Whether you're looking to boost your energy, improve your skin, support heart health, or aid in weight management, you'll find targeted recipes and information to help you achieve your objectives. One of the most transformative aspects of this book is its focus on practical, everyday use. I understand that life can be hectic, which is why I've included meal planning tips, prepahead strategies, and storage advice. You'll learn how to incorporate Nutribullet creations into your daily routine without stress or hassle.

Each recipe chapter is designed with a specific health focus in mind. From "Radiant Skin Smoothies" to "Heart Health Heroes", you'll find a wide array of delicious, nutrient-packed recipes. But more than just recipes, each chapter includes information on key ingredients and their benefits, allowing you to understand exactly how these blends are nourishing your body. I've also included a special chapter on "Superfood Sensations", introducing you to powerful ingredients that can supercharge your health. You'll learn what these superfoods are, why they're beneficial, and how to incorporate them into your daily blends.

Throughout the book, you'll find practical tips and tricks I've learned along the way. These insider secrets will help you avoid common pitfalls, save time, and get the most out of your Nutribullet. From choosing the freshest ingredients to properly storing your creations, these tips will elevate your blending game.

But perhaps the most important way this book will transform your life is by empowering you to take control of your nutrition. By the time you've worked your way through these pages, you'll have the knowledge and confidence to create your recipes, tailor blends to your taste preferences, and adapt recipes to suit your nutritional needs. Remember, this isn't about drastic diets or unrealistic health fads. The Nutribullet lifestyle is about making small, sustainable changes that add up to big results. It's about nourishing your body with whole foods, experimenting with new flavours, and finding joy in creating delicious, healthful blends.

So, whether you're looking to boost your energy, support your immune system, improve your skin, or simply incorporate more fruits and vegetables into your diet, this book is your ticket to a healthier, happier you. Get ready to blend your way to better health – your transformation starts now!

UNDERSTANDING YOUR NUTRIBULLET

PARTS AND ASSEMBLY

When I first unboxed my Nutribullet, I'll admit I was a bit overwhelmed by all the pieces. But fear not! Once you understand each component, assembly becomes a breeze. Let's break it down:

The Base
This is the powerhouse of your Nutribullet. It's where the motor sits, and it's what gives your blender its oomph. You'll notice it has a sleek design with rubber feet to keep it stable on your worktop. The top of the base has three tabs that align with the blending cup – this is key for safe operation.

The Blending Cups
Your Nutribullet likely came with a few different-sized cups. I find the tall cup perfect for most smoothies, while the short cup is brilliant for smaller portions or when I'm making dips. These cups are made of sturdy, BPA-free plastic and are dishwasher safe – a real timesaver!

The Blades
You'll have an extractor blade, which is the star of the show. It's got six prongs and is ideal for breaking down tough ingredients like nuts and seeds. Some models also come with a milling blade, which is flat and perfect for grinding dry ingredients.

The Lids
You'll have screw-on lids for storage and flip-top lids for drinking on the go. I can't tell you how many times these have saved me when I'm rushing out the door!

The Lip Rings
These fit onto the cups to give you a smooth drinking surface. They're optional, but they make sipping your creations much more comfortable.

Now, let's talk assembly. It's dead simple:
Choose your cup and fill it with ingredients.
Screw on the extractor blade.
Flip the cup upside down and align the tabs with the base.
Press down gently and twist to lock it into place.

OPERATING INSTRUCTIONS
Now that we've got our Nutribullet assembled, let's get blending! Operating this nifty machine is straightforward, but there are a few tips and tricks I've picked up along the way that'll help you get the most out of your blends.

Starting Up
Once your cup is locked into the base, you're almost ready to go. But before you start, make sure your ingredients are prepped properly. I always chop harder fruits and veg into roughly 2cm chunks – this helps them blend more smoothly and puts less strain on the motor.

The Blending Process
Here's where the magic happens! To start blending, simply press down on the cup. You'll feel it click into place. The Nutribullet will start whizzing away, breaking down your ingredients into a smooth concoction.

One of the brilliant things about the Nutribullet is that you don't need to hold a button down continuously. Once you've pressed the cup into place, it'll keep blending until you release the pressure.

Pulsing Technique
Sometimes, you might want a chunkier texture or need to dislodge an air pocket. That's where pulsing comes in handy. To pulse, press the cup down and release quickly. Repeat this action a few times until you achieve the desired consistency.

Blending Times

The time needed to blend will vary depending on your ingredients. For most smoothies, I find 30-60 seconds is plenty. For tougher ingredients like nuts or frozen fruit, you might need to blend for up to a minute and a half.

When to Stop
You'll know your blend is ready when you can't see any whole pieces of fruit or veg, and the mixture has a consistent colour and texture. If you're unsure, stop the blender, give it a little shake, and check. You can always blend for a few more seconds if needed.

Removing the Cup
Once you're happy with your blend, simply twist the cup to unlock it from the base and lift it off. Be careful – the bottom of the cup might be a bit warm from the blending process.

Remember, the Nutribullet isn't designed for hot liquids, so always let cooked ingredients cool before blending. Never run the motor for more than three minutes continuously – give it a little rest between long blends to prevent overheating.

With these tips in mind, you'll be whipping up perfect smoothies, sauces, and more in no time!

CLEANING AND MAINTENANCE
Keeping your Nutribullet clean and well-maintained is crucial for its longevity and for ensuring your blends always taste fresh. The good news is, it's a doddle to clean! Here's how I keep my Nutribullet in tiptop shape:

Immediate Rinse
The easiest way to clean your Nutribullet is to do it straight away. As soon as I've poured out my smoothie, I give the cup and blade a quick rinse under the tap. This prevents any residue from drying and becoming stubborn to remove later.

Thorough Cleaning
For a more thorough cleaning, I use warm, soapy water. The cups, lids, and lip rings can all go in the dishwasher, but I find hand washing keeps them in better condition longer. For the blades, I use a soft brush to clean around the crevices, being careful of the sharp edges.

Dealing with Tough Stains

If you've blended something particularly vibrant (like beetroot or turmeric), you might notice some staining. Don't panic! I've found that a mixture of baking soda and water, left to sit for a few minutes before scrubbing, works wonders.

Drying

After washing, I always dry everything thoroughly, especially the blades. This prevents any water spots and keeps the metal in good condition.

Cleaning the Base

The base unit can't be submerged in water, but it still needs cleaning now and then. I unplug it and wipe it down with a damp cloth, paying special attention to the area around the activator buttons where smoothie splashes might accumulate.

Blade Maintenance

The blades are the workhorses of your Nutribullet, so they need a bit of TLC. Every few months, I check them for any signs of wear or damage. If they start to look dull or chipped, it's time to replace them.

Storage

When everything's clean and dry, I store my Nutribullet components in a dry place. I usually keep the base on the worktop for easy access, with the cups and blades in a nearby cupboard.

Deep Clean

Once in a while, I give my Nutribullet a deep clean. This involves soaking the removable parts (except the blade) in warm, soapy water for about 10 minutes before scrubbing and rinsing thoroughly.

Troubleshooting and FAQs

As a longtime Nutribullet user, I've encountered my fair share of hiccups along the way. In this section, I'll share some common issues you might face and how to solve them. I'll also answer some frequently asked questions to help you get the most out of your Nutribullet experience.

COMMON ISSUES AND SOLUTIONS

THE NUTRIBULLET WON'T START

If your Nutribullet isn't powering up, try these steps:

Check that it's properly plugged in.
Ensure the cup is correctly aligned with the base.
Make sure the blade is securely attached to the cup.
If it's still not working, the safety mechanism might be engaged. Clean the activator buttons on the base and try again.

THE SMOOTHIE IS TOO THICK.

This is a common issue, especially when you're just starting. Here's what you can do:

Add more liquid to your blend.
Don't overfill past the max line.
Blend in stages, starting with the softest ingredients.

THERE ARE CHUNKS IN MY SMOOTHIE.

For a smoother blend:

Cut ingredients into smaller pieces before adding them to the cup.
Add a bit more liquid.
Blend for a longer time.
Try the pulse technique to dislodge any stuck ingredients.

THE BLADE WON'T UNSCREW FROM THE CUP.

This can happen if ingredients have dried between the blade and the cup. Try these tips:

Run the bottom of the cup under hot water for a few seconds.
Use a rubber grip to get a better hold.
If it's stuck, fill the cup with warm, soapy water and let it sit for an hour before trying again.

THERE'S A BURNING SMELL.

If you notice a burning odour:

Stop blending immediately and unplug the machine.
Check if you've overloaded the cup or blended for too long.
Allow the base to cool down before using it again.
If the smell persists, contact customer service.

FREQUENTLY ASKED QUESTIONS

Q: Can I put hot liquids in my Nutribullet?
A: No, the Nutribullet isn't designed for hot liquids. Always let ingredients cool to room temperature before blending.

Q: How long can I store my smoothies?
A: For the best taste and nutrition, consume your smoothies within 24 hours. If you need to store them longer, keep them in an airtight container in the fridge for up to 48 hours.

Q: Can I use my Nutribullet to grind coffee beans or nuts?
A: Yes, but use the milling blade for dry ingredients like these, not the extractor blade.

Q: Is it normal for the base to get warm during use?
A: A slight warmth is normal, but if it's hot to the touch, you may be overworking the motor. Try blending in shorter bursts.

Q: Can I put my Nutribullet cups in the microwave?
A: No, the cups are not microwave-safe. Always use microwave-safe containers for heating.

Q: How often should I replace the blades?
A: With regular use, blades typically last about 6 months to a year. Replace them if you notice they're becoming dull or damaged.

Q: Can I use ice in my Nutribullet?
A: Yes, but use crushed ice rather than whole cubes for better blending and to protect the blades.

Q: My Nutribullet is leaking. What should I do?
A: Check that the blade is screwed on tightly and that the rubber gasket is properly in place. If it's still leaking, the gasket might need replacing.

Remember, if you encounter any persistent issues or have concerns about your Nutribullet's performance, don't hesitate to reach out to the manufacturer's customer service. They're usually quite helpful and can provide specific advice for your model.

With these troubleshooting tips and FAQs, you should be well-equipped to handle most situations that come your way. Happy blending!!

CHAPTER 1: RADIANT SKIN SMOOTHIES

GLOWING GREEN GODDESS

Prep: 10 mins Cook: N/A Serves: 2
Blending function used: Extract

Ingredients:

US: 1 cup spinach (30g), 1/2 cup kale (15g), 1/2 avocado (75g), 1 green apple (chopped, 180g), 1/2 cucumber (chopped, 100g), 1 tablespoon lemon juice (15ml), 1 cup coconut water (240ml)

UK: 30g spinach, 15g kale, 75g avocado (1/2), 180g green apple (chopped), 100g cucumber (chopped, 1/2), 15ml lemon juice, 240ml coconut water

Instructions:

Add the spinach, kale, avocado, green apple, cucumber, lemon juice, and coconut water into the Nutribullet.

Secure the lid and blend on the 'Extract' setting until smooth.

Pour into two glasses and enjoy your Glowing Green Goddess smoothie immediately for a refreshing start to your day.

Nutritional Info: Calories: 150 Fat: 7g Carbs: 20g Protein: 2g

BERRY COLLAGEN BOOSTER

Prep: 5 mins Cook: N/A Serves: 2
Blending function used: Extract

Ingredients:

US: 1 cup mixed berries (150g), 1 banana (120g), 1 scoop collagen powder (10g), 1 cup almond milk (240ml), 1 tablespoon chia seeds (12g)

UK: 150g mixed berries, 120g banana, 10g collagen powder (1 scoop), 240ml almond milk, 12g chia seeds (1 tablespoon)

Instructions:

Combine the mixed berries, banana, collagen powder, almond milk, and chia seeds in your Nutribullet.

Blend on the 'Extract' setting until everything is fully mixed and smooth.

Pour into glasses and serve immediately for a nutritious and skin-loving smoothie.

Nutritional Info: Calories: 200 Fat: 5g Carbs: 35g Protein: 10g

CUCUMBER MINT REFRESHER

Prep: 10 mins Cook: N/A Serves: 2

Blending function used: Extract

Ingredients:

US: 1 cucumber (200g, peeled and chopped), 1/4 cup fresh mint leaves (10g), 1 lime (juiced, 30ml), 1 tablespoon honey (15g), 1 cup water (240ml), ice cubes

UK: 200g cucumber (peeled and chopped), 10g fresh mint leaves (1/4 cup), 30ml lime juice (1 lime), 15g honey (1 tablespoon), 240ml water, ice cubes

Instructions:

Place the cucumber, fresh mint leaves, lime juice, honey, and water into the Nutribullet.

Blend on the 'Extract' setting until smooth.

Add ice cubes to your glasses, pour over the mixture, and serve chilled for a refreshing drink.

Nutritional Info: Calories: 80 Fat: 0g Carbs: 20g Protein: 1g

CARROT GINGER GLOW

Prep: 10 mins Cook: N/A Serves: 2

Blending function used: Extract

Ingredients:

US: 2 large carrots (200g, peeled and chopped), 1 orange (peeled), 1inch piece ginger (5g, peeled), 1/2 cup Greek yoghurt (120g), 1 cup orange juice (240ml)

UK: 200g large carrots (peeled and chopped), 1 orange (peeled), 5g ginger (1inch piece, peeled), 120g Greek yoghurt (1/2 cup), 240ml orange juice

Instructions:

Add the carrots, orange, ginger, Greek yoghurt, and orange juice to the Nutribullet.

Blend on the 'Extract' setting until smooth and creamy.

Serve immediately in glasses for a vibrant, glowing smoothie.

Nutritional Info: Calories: 170 Fat: 3g Carbs: 32g Protein: 5g

AVOCADO SPINACH HYDRATOR

Prep: 10 mins Cook: N/A Serves: 2
Blending function used: Extract

Ingredients:

US: 1 avocado (150g), 1 cup spinach (30g), 1 green apple (chopped, 180g), 1/2 cup coconut milk (120ml), 1 cup water (240ml)

UK: 150g avocado (1), 30g spinach (1 cup), 180g green apple (chopped), 120ml coconut milk (1/2 cup), 240ml water

Instructions:

Place the avocado, spinach, green apple, coconut milk, and water into the Nutribullet.
Blend on the 'Extract' setting until well-mixed and smooth.
Pour into glasses and enjoy immediately for a hydrating and nutritious smoothie.

Nutritional Info: Calories: 250 Fat: 18g Carbs: 20g Protein: 3g

POMEGRANATE ANTIOXIDANT BLAST

Prep: 5 mins Cook: N/A Serves: 2
Blending function used: Extract

Ingredients:

US: 1 cup pomegranate seeds (150g), 1 cup blueberries (150g), 1 banana (120g), 1/2 cup Greek yoghurt (120g), 1 cup water (240ml)

UK: 150g pomegranate seeds (1 cup), 150g blueberries (1 cup), 120g banana (1), 120g Greek yoghurt (1/2 cup), 240ml water

Instructions:

Combine the pomegranate seeds, blueberries, banana, Greek yoghurt, and water in the Nutribullet.
Blend on the 'Extract' setting until smooth and creamy.
Serve immediately in glasses for a burst of antioxidants.

Nutritional Info: Calories: 200 Fat: 3g Carbs: 40g Protein: 6g

KIWI VITAMIN C KICK

Prep: 5 mins Cook: N/A Serves: 2

Blending function used: Extract

Ingredients:

US: 3 kiwis (peeled, 200g), 1 orange (peeled), 1/2 cup Greek yoghurt (120g), 1 cup water (240ml)

UK: 200g kiwis (peeled, 3), 1 orange (peeled), 120g Greek yoghurt (1/2 cup), 240ml water

Instructions:

Add the kiwis, orange, Greek yoghurt, and water to the Nutribullet.

Blend on the 'Extract' setting until smooth.

Pour into glasses and enjoy immediately for a vitamin C boost.

Nutritional Info: Calories: 150 Fat: 2g Carbs: 30g Protein: 5g

PAPAYA ENZYME ELIXIR

Prep: 5 mins Cook: N/A Serves: 2

Blending function used: Extract

Ingredients:

US: 1 cup papaya (150g, peeled and chopped), 1 banana (120g), 1/2 cup Greek yoghurt (120g), 1 cup coconut water (240ml)

UK: 150g papaya (peeled and chopped, 1 cup), 120g banana (1), 120g Greek yoghurt (1/2 cup), 240ml coconut water

Instructions:

Combine the papaya, banana, Greek yoghurt, and coconut water in the Nutribullet.

Blend on the 'Extract' setting until smooth and creamy.

Serve immediately in glasses for a refreshing enzyme-packed smoothie.

Nutritional Info: Calories: 180 Fat: 3g Carbs: 35g Protein: 6g

ALOE VERA SKIN SOOTHER

Prep: 5 mins Cook: N/A Serves: 2
Blending function used: Extract

Ingredients:

US: 1/4 cup aloe vera gel (60ml), 1 cucumber (200g, peeled and chopped), 1 green apple (chopped, 180g), 1 cup coconut water (240ml)

UK: 60ml aloe vera gel (1/4 cup), 200g cucumber (peeled and chopped, 1), 180g green apple (chopped, 1), 240ml coconut water

Instructions:

Add the aloe vera gel, cucumber, green apple, and coconut water into the Nutribullet.
Blend on the 'Extract' setting until smooth.
Pour into glasses and enjoy immediately for a soothing skin-friendly drink.

Nutritional Info: Calories: 100 Fat: 0g Carbs: 25g Protein: 1g

BEETROOT BEAUTY BLEND

Prep: 10 mins Cook: N/A Serves: 2
Blending function used: Extract

Ingredients:

US: 1 small beetroot (100g, peeled and chopped), 1 apple (chopped, 180g), 1 carrot (100g, peeled and chopped), 1 tablespoon lemon juice (15ml), 1 cup water (240ml)

UK: 100g beetroot (small, peeled and chopped), 180g apple (chopped, 1), 100g carrot (peeled and chopped, 1), 15ml lemon juice (1 tablespoon), 240ml water

Instructions:

Place the beetroot, apple, carrot, lemon juice, and water into the Nutribullet.
Blend on the 'Extract' setting until smooth.
Serve immediately in glasses for a vibrant and nutritious drink.

Nutritional Info: Calories: 110 Fat: 0g Carbs: 25g Protein: 2g

MANGO TURMERIC RADIANCE

Prep: 10 mins Cook: N/A Serves: 2
Blending function used: Extract

Ingredients:

US: 1 cup mango (150g, peeled and chopped), 1/2 teaspoon turmeric powder (2.5g), 1/2 cup Greek yoghurt (120g), 1 cup coconut water (240ml)

UK: 150g mango (peeled and chopped, 1 cup), 2.5g turmeric powder (1/2 teaspoon), 120g Greek yoghurt (1/2 cup), 240ml coconut water

Instructions:

Combine the mango, turmeric powder, Greek yoghurt, and coconut water in the Nutribullet.

Blend on the 'Extract' setting until smooth.

Pour into glasses and enjoy immediately for a radiant and healthy smoothie.

Nutritional Info: Calories: 160 Fat: 3g Carbs: 30g Protein: 6g

BLUEBERRY ACAI SKIN SHIELD

Prep: 5 mins Cook: N/A Serves: 2
Blending function used: Extract

Ingredients:

US: 1 cup blueberries (150g), 1 tablespoon acai powder (10g), 1 banana (120g), 1/2 cup almond milk (120ml), 1 cup water (240ml)

UK: 150g blueberries (1 cup), 10g acai powder (1 tablespoon), 120g banana (1), 120ml almond milk (1/2 cup), 240ml water

Instructions:

Add the blueberries, acai powder, banana, almond milk, and water to the Nutribullet.

Blend on the 'Extract' setting until smooth.

Serve immediately in glasses for a skin-protecting smoothie.

Nutritional Info: Calories: 180 Fat: 2g Carbs: 38g Protein: 3g

COCONUT WATER COMPLEXION CLEARER

Prep: 5 mins Cook: N/A Serves: 2

Blending function used: Extract

Ingredients:

US: 1 cup coconut water (240ml), 1 cucumber (200g, peeled and chopped), 1 green apple (chopped, 180g), 1 tablespoon lemon juice (15ml), ice cubes

UK: 240ml coconut water (1 cup), 200g cucumber (peeled and chopped, 1), 180g green apple (chopped, 1), 15ml lemon juice (1 tablespoon), ice cubes

Instructions:

Combine the coconut water, cucumber, green apple, and lemon juice in the Nutribullet.

Blend on the 'Extract' setting until smooth.

Pour over ice cubes in glasses and serve immediately for a refreshing and complexion-clearing drink.

Nutritional Info: Calories: 90 Fat: 0g Carbs: 22g Protein: 1g

CHAPTER 2: ANTIAGING ELIXIRS

BERRY AGEDEFYING BLEND

Prep: 5 mins Cook: N/A Serves: 2

Blending function used: Extract

Ingredients:

US: 1 cup mixed berries (150g), 1 banana (120g), 1 cup spinach (30g), 1 tablespoon chia seeds (12g), 1 cup almond milk (240ml)

UK: 150g mixed berries, 120g banana, 30g spinach (1 cup), 12g chia seeds (1 tablespoon), 240ml almond milk

Instructions:

Add the mixed berries, banana, spinach, chia seeds, and almond milk into your Nutribullet.

Secure the lid and blend on the 'Extract' setting until smooth.

Pour into two glasses and enjoy your Berry Age Defying Blend immediately.

Nutritional Info: Calories: 200 Fat: 6g Carbs: 36g Protein: 5g

GREEN TEA ANTIOXIDANT SMOOTHIE

Prep: 5 mins Cook: N/A Serves: 2

Blending function used: Extract

Ingredients:

US: 1 cup green tea (240ml, cooled), 1 cup spinach (30g), 1/2 avocado (75g), 1 apple (chopped, 180g), 1 tablespoon honey (15g)

UK: 240ml green tea (cooled, 1 cup), 30g spinach (1 cup), 75g avocado (1/2), 180g apple (chopped, 1), 15g honey (1 tablespoon)

Instructions:

Place the green tea, spinach, avocado, apple, and honey into the Nutribullet.

Blend on the 'Extract' setting until smooth and creamy.

Serve immediately in glasses for a refreshing antioxidant boost.

Nutritional Info: Calories: 150 Fat: 7g Carbs: 25g Protein: 2g

CACAO NIB YOUTH BOOSTER

Prep: 5 mins Cook: N/A Serves: 2

Blending function used: Extract

Ingredients:

US: 1 banana (120g), 1 tablespoon cacao nibs (15g), 1/2 cup Greek yoghurt (120g), 1 cup almond milk (240ml), 1 tablespoon honey (15g)

UK: 120g banana (1), 15g cacao nibs (1 tablespoon), 120g Greek yoghurt (1/2 cup), 240ml almond milk, 15g honey (1 tablespoon)

Instructions:

Combine the banana, cacao nibs, Greek yoghurt, almond milk, and honey in the Nutribullet.

Blend on the 'Extract' setting until smooth.

Pour into glasses and enjoy your Cacao Nib Youth Booster smoothie right away.

Nutritional Info: Calories: 220 Fat: 6g Carbs: 38g Protein: 8g

OMEGA3 RICH FLAXSEED SHAKE

Prep: 5 mins Cook: N/A Serves: 2

Blending function used: Extract

Ingredients:

US: 1 tablespoon flaxseed (10g), 1 banana (120g), 1 cup blueberries (150g), 1 cup spinach (30g), 1 cup water (240ml)

UK: 10g flaxseed (1 tablespoon), 120g banana (1), 150g blueberries (1 cup), 30g spinach (1 cup), 240ml water

Instructions:

Add the flaxseed, banana, blueberries, spinach, and water into your Nutribullet.

Blend on the 'Extract' setting until smooth.

Pour into glasses and enjoy your Omega3 Rich Flaxseed Shake immediately.

Nutritional Info: Calories: 180 Fat: 4g Carbs: 35g Protein: 4g

SPIRULINA SUPERFOOD ELIXIR

Prep: 5 mins Cook: N/A Serves: 2
Blending function used: Extract

Ingredients:

US: 1 teaspoon spirulina powder (5g), 1 banana (120g), 1/2 cup pineapple (75g), 1 cup coconut water (240ml), 1 tablespoon chia seeds (12g)

UK: 5g spirulina powder (1 teaspoon), 120g banana (1), 75g pineapple (1/2 cup), 240ml coconut water (1 cup), 12g chia seeds (1 tablespoon)

Instructions:

Place the spirulina powder, banana, pineapple, coconut water, and chia seeds into the Nutribullet. Blend on the 'Extract' setting until smooth.

Serve immediately in glasses for a nutritious superfood elixir.

Nutritional Info: Calories: 160 Fat: 3g Carbs: 32g Protein: 4g

POMEGRANATE SEED REJUVENATOR

Prep: 5 mins Cook: N/A Serves: 2
Blending function used: Extract

Ingredients:

US: 1 cup pomegranate seeds (150g), 1 cup strawberries (150g), 1 banana (120g), 1/2 cup Greek yoghurt (120g), 1 cup water (240ml)

UK: 150g pomegranate seeds (1 cup), 150g strawberries (1 cup), 120g banana (1), 120g Greek yoghurt (1/2 cup), 240ml water

Instructions:

Add the pomegranate seeds, strawberries, banana, Greek yoghurt, and water into your Nutribullet. Blend on the 'Extract' setting until smooth.

Pour into glasses and enjoy your Pomegranate Seed Rejuvenator immediately.

Nutritional Info: Calories: 180 Fat: 3g Carbs: 38g Protein: 6g

KALE AND ALMOND ANTIWRINKLE BLEND

Prep: 5 mins Cook: N/A Serves: 2

Blending function used: Extract

Ingredients:

US: 1 cup kale (30g), 1/4 cup almonds (30g), 1 banana (120g), 1/2 cup Greek yoghurt (120g), 1 cup almond milk (240ml)

UK: 30g kale (1 cup), 30g almonds (1/4 cup), 120g banana (1), 120g Greek yoghurt (1/2 cup), 240ml almond milk

Instructions:

Combine the kale, almonds, banana, Greek yoghurt, and almond milk in the Nutribullet.
Blend on the 'Extract' setting until smooth and creamy.
Serve immediately in glasses for an antiwrinkle boost.

Nutritional Info: Calories: 250 Fat: 12g Carbs: 30g Protein: 10g

GOJI BERRY LONGEVITY TONIC

Prep: 5 mins Cook: N/A Serves: 2

Blending function used: Extract

Ingredients:

US: 1/4 cup goji berries (30g), 1 cup strawberries (150g), 1 banana (120g), 1 cup coconut water (240ml)

UK: 30g goji berries (1/4 cup), 150g strawberries (1 cup), 120g banana (1), 240ml coconut water (1 cup)

Instructions:

Place the goji berries, strawberries, bananas, and coconut water into the Nutribullet.
Blend on the 'Extract' setting until smooth.
Pour into glasses and enjoy your Goji Berry Longevity Tonic immediately.

Nutritional Info: Calories: 170 Fat: 1g Carbs: 40g Protein: 4g

AVOCADO EBOOSTER SMOOTHIE

Prep: 5 mins Cook: N/A Serves: 2

Blending function used: Extract

Ingredients:

US: 1/2 avocado (75g), 1 cup spinach (30g), 1 banana (120g), 1 tablespoon flaxseed (10g), 1 cup almond milk (240ml)

UK: 75g avocado (1/2), 30g spinach (1 cup), 120g banana (1), 10g flaxseed (1 tablespoon), 240ml almond milk

Instructions:

Add the avocado, spinach, banana, flaxseed, and almond milk into your Nutribullet.

Blend on the 'Extract' setting until smooth.

Serve immediately in glasses for a vitamin E boost.

Nutritional Info: Calories: 210 Fat: 12g Carbs: 24g Protein: 5g

COLLAGENSUPPORTING CITRUS BLEND

Prep: 5 mins Cook: N/A Serves: 2

Blending function used: Extract

Ingredients:

US: 1 orange (peeled), 1/2 grapefruit (peeled), 1/2 lemon (peeled), 1 tablespoon chia seeds (12g), 1 cup water (240ml)

UK: 1 orange (peeled), 1/2 grapefruit (peeled), 1/2 lemon (peeled), 12g chia seeds (1 tablespoon), 240ml water

Instructions:

Place the orange, grapefruit, lemon, chia seeds, and water into the Nutribullet.

Blend on the 'Extract' setting until smooth.

Pour into glasses and enjoy your Collagen Supporting Citrus Blend immediately.

Nutritional Info: Calories: 100 Fat: 3g Carbs: 24g Protein: 2g

RESVERATROLRICH RED GRAPE SMOOTHIE

Prep: 5 mins Cook: N/A Serves: 2

Blending function used: Extract

Ingredients:

US: 1 cup red grapes (150g), 1 apple (chopped, 180g), 1/2 cup Greek yoghurt (120g), 1 tablespoon honey (15g), 1 cup water (240ml)

UK: 150g red grapes (1 cup), 180g apple (chopped, 1), 120g Greek yoghurt (1/2 cup), 15g honey (1 tablespoon), 240ml water

Instructions:

Add the red grapes, apple, Greek yoghurt, honey, and water into the Nutribullet.

Blend on the 'Extract' setting until smooth.

Serve immediately in glasses for a resveratrol boost.

Nutritional Info: Calories: 170 Fat: 2g Carbs: 38g Protein: 6g

MATCHA GREEN TEA ENERGY LIFT

Prep: 5 mins Cook: N/A Serves: 2

Blending function used: Extract

Ingredients:

US: 1 teaspoon matcha powder (5g), 1 banana (120g), 1/2 cup Greek yoghurt (120g), 1 cup almond milk (240ml), 1 tablespoon honey (15g)

UK: 5g matcha powder (1 teaspoon), 120g banana (1), 120g Greek yoghurt (1/2 cup), 240ml almond milk, 15g honey (1 tablespoon)

Instructions:

Place the matcha powder, banana, Greek yoghurt, almond milk, and honey into the Nutribullet. Blend on the 'Extract' setting until smooth and creamy.

Serve immediately in glasses for an energising lift.

Nutritional Info: Calories: 190 Fat: 4g Carbs: 33g Protein: 7g

AÇAI BERRY AGEREVERSAL BLEND

Prep: 5 mins Cook: N/A Serves: 2
Blending function used: Extract

Ingredients:

US: 1 tablespoon açai powder (10g), 1 cup blueberries (150g), 1 banana (120g), 1/2 cup Greek yoghurt (120g), 1 cup almond milk (240ml)

UK: 10g açai powder (1 tablespoon), 150g blueberries (1 cup), 120g banana (1), 120g Greek yoghurt (1/2 cup), 240ml almond milk

Instructions:

Add the açai powder, blueberries, banana, Greek yoghurt, and almond milk into the Nutribullet.
Blend on the 'Extract' setting until smooth.
Serve immediately in glasses for an age-reversing treat.

Nutritional Info: Calories: 200 Fat: 4g Carbs: 38g Protein: 7g

CHAPTER 3: DETOX AND CLEANSE SMOOTHIES

GREEN DETOX DREAM

Prep: 5 mins Cook: N/A Serves: 2

Blending function used: Extract

Ingredients:

US: 1 cup kale (30g), 1 apple (chopped, 180g), 1/2 cucumber (75g), 1 lemon (juiced), 1 cup coconut water (240ml)

UK: 30g kale (1 cup), 180g apple (chopped, 1), 75g cucumber (1/2), 1 lemon (juiced), 240ml coconut water

Instructions:

Add the kale, apple, cucumber, lemon juice, and coconut water to your Nutribullet.

Secure the lid and blend on the 'Extract' setting until smooth.

Pour into two glasses and enjoy your Green Detox Dream immediately.

Nutritional Info: Calories: 70 Fat: 0g Carbs: 17g Protein: 1g

LEMON GINGER FLUSH

Prep: 5 mins Cook: N/A Serves: 2

Blending function used: Extract

Ingredients:

US: 1 lemon (juiced), 1inch ginger (2.5cm), 1 apple (chopped, 180g), 1 cup water (240ml), 1 tablespoon honey (15g)

UK: 1 lemon (juiced), 2.5cm ginger (1 inch), 180g apple (chopped, 1), 240ml water, 15g honey (1 tablespoon)

Instructions:

Place the lemon juice, ginger, apple, water, and honey into the Nutribullet.

Blend on the 'Extract' setting until smooth.

Serve immediately in glasses for a refreshing flush.

Nutritional Info: Calories: 80 Fat: 0g Carbs: 21g Protein: 1g

ACTIVATED CHARCOAL CLEANSE

Prep: 5 mins Cook: N/A Serves: 2
Blending function used: Extract

Ingredients:

US: 1 teaspoon activated charcoal (5g), 1 banana (120g), 1 cup almond milk (240ml), 1 tablespoon honey (15g)

UK: 5g activated charcoal (1 teaspoon), 120g banana (1), 240ml almond milk, 15g honey (1 tablespoon)

Instructions:

Combine the activated charcoal, banana, almond milk, and honey in the Nutribullet.
Blend on the 'Extract' setting until smooth.
Pour into glasses and enjoy your Activated Charcoal Cleanse immediately.

Nutritional Info: Calories: 120 Fat: 3g Carbs: 23g Protein: 2g

BEET AND BERRY LIVER SUPPORT

Prep: 5 mins Cook: N/A Serves: 2
Blending function used: Extract

Ingredients:

US: 1 small beetroot (peeled and chopped, 100g), 1/2 cup strawberries (75g), 1/2 cup blueberries (75g), 1 cup water (240ml)

UK: 100g beetroot (peeled and chopped, 1 small), 75g strawberries (1/2 cup), 75g blueberries (1/2 cup), 240ml water

Instructions:

Add the beetroot, strawberries, blueberries, and water into your Nutribullet.
Blend on the 'Extract' setting until smooth.
Serve immediately in glasses for a liver-supporting boost.

Nutritional Info: Calories: 80 Fat: 0g Carbs: 19g Protein: 2g

CILANTRO CHELATION BLEND

Prep: 5 mins Cook: N/A Serves: 2
Blending function used: Extract

Ingredients:

US: 1 cup cilantro (30g), 1 apple (chopped, 180g), 1/2 cucumber (75g), 1 lime (juiced), 1 cup water (240ml)

UK: 30g cilantro (1 cup), 180g apple (chopped, 1), 75g cucumber (1/2), 1 lime (juiced), 240ml water

Instructions:

Combine the cilantro, apple, cucumber, lime juice, and water in the Nutribullet.
Blend on the 'Extract' setting until smooth.
Serve immediately in glasses for a chelation boost.

Nutritional Info: Calories: 50 Fat: 0g Carbs: 13g Protein: 1g

DANDELION GREENS DETOXIFIER

Prep: 5 mins Cook: N/A Serves: 2
Blending function used: Extract

Ingredients:

US: 1 cup dandelion greens (30g), 1/2 cup pineapple (75g), 1 apple (chopped, 180g), 1 cup coconut water (240ml)

UK: 30g dandelion greens (1 cup), 75g pineapple (1/2 cup), 180g apple (chopped, 1), 240ml coconut water

Instructions:

Add the dandelion greens, pineapple, apple, and coconut water into your Nutribullet.
Blend on the 'Extract' setting until smooth.
Serve immediately in glasses for a detoxifying treat.

Nutritional Info: Calories: 70 Fat: 0g Carbs: 18g Protein: 1g

WATERMELON FLUSH

Prep: 5 mins Cook: N/A Serves: 2

Blending function used: Extract

Ingredients:

US: 2 cups watermelon (300g), 1/2 cucumber (75g), 1 lime (juiced), 1 cup water (240ml)
UK: 300g watermelon (2 cups), 75g cucumber (1/2), 1 lime (juiced), 240ml water

Instructions:

Combine the watermelon, cucumber, lime juice, and water in the Nutribullet.
Blend on the 'Extract' setting until smooth.
Serve immediately in glasses for a refreshing flush.

Nutritional Info: Calories: 60 Fat: 0g Carbs: 15g Protein: 1g

PINEAPPLE ENZYME CLEANSER

Prep: 5 mins Cook: N/A Serves: 2

Blending function used: Extract

Ingredients:

US: 1 cup pineapple (150g), 1/2 cucumber (75g), 1/2 lemon (juiced), 1 cup coconut water (240ml)
UK: 150g pineapple (1 cup), 75g cucumber (1/2), 1/2 lemon (juiced), 240ml coconut water

Instructions:

Add the pineapple, cucumber, lemon juice, and coconut water to your Nutribullet.
Blend on the 'Extract' setting until smooth.
Serve immediately in glasses for an enzyme cleanse.

Nutritional Info: Calories: 70 Fat: 0g Carbs: 17g Protein: 1g

CHLORELLA CLEAROUT

Prep: 5 mins Cook: N/A Serves: 2

Blending function used: Extract

Ingredients:

US: 1 teaspoon chlorella powder (5g), 1 banana (120g), 1 apple (chopped, 180g), 1 cup water (240ml)
UK: 5g chlorella powder (1 teaspoon), 120g banana (1), 180g apple (chopped, 1), 240ml water

Instructions:

Combine the chlorella powder, banana, apple, and water in the Nutribullet.
Blend on the 'Extract' setting until smooth.
Serve immediately in glasses for a clear-out cleanse.

Nutritional Info: Calories: 80 Fat: 0g Carbs: 20g Protein: 1g

CRANBERRY KIDNEY CLEANSE

Prep: 5 mins Cook: N/A Serves: 2

Blending function used: Extract

Ingredients:

US: 1/2 cup cranberries (75g), 1 apple (chopped, 180g), 1/2 cucumber (75g), 1 cup water (240ml)
UK: 75g cranberries (1/2 cup), 180g apple (chopped, 1), 75g cucumber (1/2), 240ml water

Instructions:

Add the cranberries, apple, cucumber, and water into your Nutribullet.
Blend on the 'Extract' setting until smooth.
Serve immediately in glasses for a kidney cleanse.

Nutritional Info: Calories: 60 Fat: 0g Carbs: 15g Protein: 1g

APPLE CIDER VINEGAR DETOX

Prep: 5 mins Cook: N/A Serves: 2
Blending function used: Extract

Ingredients:

US: 2 tablespoons apple cider vinegar (30ml), 1 apple (chopped, 180g), 1 tablespoon honey (15g), 1 cup water (240ml)

UK: 30ml apple cider vinegar (2 tablespoons), 180g apple (chopped, 1), 15g honey (1 tablespoon), 240ml water

Instructions:

Place the apple cider vinegar, apple, honey, and water into the Nutribullet.

Blend on the 'Extract' setting until smooth.

Serve immediately in glasses for a detoxifying boost.

Nutritional Info: Calories: 70 Fat: 0g Carbs: 18g Protein: 0g

TURMERIC GOLDEN MILK DETOXIFIER

Prep: 5 mins Cook: N/A Serves: 2
Blending function used: Extract

Ingredients:

US: 1 teaspoon turmeric powder (5g), 1 cup almond milk (240ml), 1 banana (120g), 1 tablespoon honey (15g)

UK: 5g turmeric powder (1 teaspoon), 240ml almond milk (1 cup), 120g banana (1), 15g honey (1 tablespoon)

Instructions:

Combine the turmeric powder, almond milk, banana, and honey in the Nutribullet.

Blend on the 'Extract' setting until smooth.

Serve immediately in glasses for a golden detox.

Nutritional Info: Calories: 120 Fat: 3g Carbs: 25g Protein: 2g

PARSLEY AND CELERY JUICE BLEND

Prep: 5 mins Cook: N/A Serves: 2

Blending function used: Extract

Ingredients:

US: 1 cup parsley (30g), 2 stalks celery (200g), 1 apple (chopped, 180g), 1/2 lemon (juiced), 1 cup water (240ml)

UK: 30g parsley (1 cup), 200g celery (2 stalks), 180g apple (chopped, 1), 1/2 lemon (juiced), 240ml water

Instructions:

Add the parsley, celery, apple, lemon juice, and water to your Nutribullet.

Blend on the 'Extract' setting until smooth.

Serve immediately in glasses for a cleansing boost.

Nutritional Info: Calories: 70 Fat: 0g Carbs: 17g Protein: 1g

CHAPTER 4: WEIGHT LOSS WONDERS

GREEN METABOLISM BOOSTER

Prep: 5 mins Cook: N/A Serves: 2

Blending function used: Extract

Ingredients:

US: 1 cup spinach (30g), 1/2 cucumber (75g), 1 green apple (180g), 1 teaspoon matcha powder (5g), 1 cup coconut water (240ml)

UK: 30g spinach (1 cup), 75g cucumber (1/2), 180g green apple (1), 5g matcha powder (1 teaspoon), 240ml coconut water

Instructions:

Add the spinach, cucumber, green apple, matcha powder, and coconut water to your Nutribullet. Blend on the 'Extract' setting until smooth.

Pour into two glasses and enjoy your Green Metabolism Booster immediately.

Nutritional Info: Calories: 70 Fat: 0g Carbs: 18g Protein: 1g

BERRY PROTEIN PUNCH

Prep: 5 mins Cook: N/A Serves: 2

Blending function used: Extract

Ingredients:

US: 1/2 cup strawberries (75g), 1/2 cup blueberries (75g), 1/2 cup Greek yoghurt (120g), 1 tablespoon chia seeds (15g), 1 cup almond milk (240ml)

UK: 75g strawberries (1/2 cup), 75g blueberries (1/2 cup), 120g Greek yoghurt (1/2 cup), 15g chia seeds (1 tablespoon), 240ml almond milk

Instructions:

Combine the strawberries, blueberries, Greek yoghurt, chia seeds, and almond milk in the Nutribullet.

Blend on the 'Extract' setting until smooth.

Serve immediately in two glasses for a protein-packed punch.

Nutritional Info: Calories: 150 Fat: 5g Carbs: 19g Protein: 9g

CINNAMON ROLL PROTEIN SHAKE

Prep: 5 mins Cook: N/A Serves: 2

Blending function used: Extract

Ingredients:

US: 1 scoop vanilla protein powder (30g), 1/2 teaspoon cinnamon (2g), 1 banana (120g), 1 cup almond milk (240ml), 1 tablespoon almond butter (15g)

UK: 30g vanilla protein powder (1 scoop), 2g cinnamon (1/2 teaspoon), 120g banana (1), 240ml almond milk, 15g almond butter (1 tablespoon)

Instructions:

Add the protein powder, cinnamon, banana, almond milk, and almond butter to the Nutribullet.

Blend on the 'Extract' setting until smooth.

Serve immediately in two glasses for a cinnamon roll-inspired treat.

Nutritional Info: Calories: 250 Fat: 10g Carbs: 25g Protein: 15g

SPINACH AND PEAR SLIMMER

Prep: 5 mins Cook: N/A Serves: 2

Blending function used: Extract

Ingredients:

US: 1 cup spinach (30g), 1 pear (chopped, 150g), 1/2 avocado (75g), 1 cup water (240ml), 1 tablespoon lemon juice (15ml)

UK: 30g spinach (1 cup), 150g pear (chopped, 1), 75g avocado (1/2), 240ml water, 15ml lemon juice (1 tablespoon)

Instructions:

Combine the spinach, pear, avocado, water, and lemon juice in the Nutribullet.

Blend on the 'Extract' setting until smooth.

Serve immediately in two glasses for a refreshing slimming smoothie.

Nutritional Info: Calories: 90 Fat: 4g Carbs: 16g Protein: 1g

CHIA SEED FILLING SMOOTHIE

Prep: 5 mins Cook: N/A Serves: 2
Blending function used: Extract

Ingredients:

US: 1 tablespoon chia seeds (15g), 1 banana (120g), 1/2 cup Greek yoghurt (120g), 1 cup almond milk (240ml), 1 teaspoon honey (5g)

UK: 15g chia seeds (1 tablespoon), 120g banana (1), 120g Greek yoghurt (1/2 cup), 240ml almond milk, 5g honey (1 teaspoon)

Instructions:

Add the chia seeds, banana, Greek yoghurt, almond milk, and honey to your Nutribullet.
Blend on the 'Extract' setting until smooth.
Pour into two glasses and enjoy your filling chia seed smoothie immediately.

Nutritional Info: Calories: 200 Fat: 6g Carbs: 30g Protein: 8g

GRAPEFRUIT FAT BURNER

Prep: 5 mins Cook: N/A Serves: 2
Blending function used: Extract

Ingredients:

US: 1 grapefruit (peeled and segmented, 230g), 1/2 cup pineapple (75g), 1/2 cucumber (75g), 1 cup water (240ml)

UK: 230g grapefruit (peeled and segmented, 1), 75g pineapple (1/2 cup), 75g cucumber (1/2), 240ml water

Instructions:

Place the grapefruit, pineapple, cucumber, and water into the Nutribullet.
Blend on the 'Extract' setting until smooth.
Serve immediately in two glasses for a fat-burning boost.

Nutritional Info: Calories: 60 Fat: 0g Carbs: 15g Protein: 1g

CHOCOLATE PB2 PROTEIN SHAKE

Prep: 5 mins Cook: N/A Serves: 2

Blending function used: Extract

Ingredients:

US: 1 scoop chocolate protein powder (30g), 2 tablespoons PB2 powder (12g), 1 banana (120g), 1 cup almond milk (240ml)

UK: 30g chocolate protein powder (1 scoop), 12g PB2 powder (2 tablespoons), 120g banana (1), 240ml almond milk

Instructions:

Combine the chocolate protein powder, PB2 powder, banana, and almond milk in the Nutribullet.

Blend on the 'Extract' setting until smooth.

Serve immediately in two glasses for a chocolatey protein boost.

Nutritional Info: Calories: 220 Fat: 4g Carbs: 30g Protein: 15g

CAYENNE KICKSTART BLEND

Prep: 5 mins Cook: N/A Serves: 2

Blending function used: Extract

Ingredients:

US: 1/2 teaspoon cayenne pepper (2g), 1 lemon (juiced), 1 apple (chopped, 180g), 1 cup water (240ml), 1 teaspoon honey (5g)

UK: 2g cayenne pepper (1/2 teaspoon), 1 lemon (juiced), 180g apple (chopped, 1), 240ml water, 5g honey (1 teaspoon)

Instructions:

Add the cayenne pepper, lemon juice, apple, water, and honey to the Nutribullet.

Blend on the 'Extract' setting until smooth.

Serve immediately in two glasses for a spicy kickstart to your day.

Nutritional Info: Calories: 50 Fat: 0g Carbs: 13g Protein: 0g

MATCHA GREEN TEA FAT BURNER

Prep: 5 mins Cook: N/A Serves: 2
Blending function used: Extract
Ingredients:
US: 1 teaspoon matcha powder (5g), 1 banana (120g), 1 cup almond milk (240ml), 1 tablespoon honey (15g)
UK: 5g matcha powder (1 teaspoon), 120g banana (1), 240ml almond milk, 15g honey (1 tablespoon)
Instructions:
Combine the matcha powder, banana, almond milk, and honey in the Nutribullet.
Blend on the 'Extract' setting until smooth.
Serve immediately in two glasses for a metabolism-boosting drink.
Nutritional Info: Calories: 140 Fat: 3g Carbs: 28g Protein: 2g

CELERY AND APPLE FLAT BELLY SMOOTHER

Prep: 5 mins Cook: N/A Serves: 2
Blending function used: Extract
Ingredients:
US: 2 stalks celery (200g), 1 apple (chopped, 180g), 1/2 lemon (juiced), 1 cup water (240ml)
UK: 200g celery (2 stalks), 180g apple (chopped, 1), 1/2 lemon (juiced), 240ml water
Instructions:
Add the celery, apple, lemon juice, and water to the Nutribullet.
Blend on the 'Extract' setting until smooth.
Serve immediately in two glasses for a flat belly smoother.
Nutritional Info: Calories: 50 Fat: 0g Carbs: 13g Protein: 0g

PINEAPPLE COCONUT METABOLISM BOOSTER

Prep: 5 mins Cook: N/A Serves: 2
Blending function used: Extract

Ingredients:

US: 1/2 cup pineapple (75g), 1/2 cup coconut milk (120ml), 1 banana (120g), 1 teaspoon honey (5g)
UK: 75g pineapple (1/2 cup), 120ml coconut milk (1/2 cup), 120g banana (1), 5g honey (1 teaspoon)

Instructions:

Combine the pineapple, coconut milk, banana, and honey in the Nutribullet.
Blend on the 'Extract' setting until smooth.
Serve immediately in two glasses for a tropical metabolism boost.

Nutritional Info: Calories: 180 Fat: 7g Carbs: 30g Protein: 2g

RASPBERRY KETONE KICKER

Prep: 5 mins Cook: N/A Serves: 2
Blending function used: Extract

Ingredients:
US: 1/2 cup raspberries (75g), 1 teaspoon raspberry ketone powder (5g), 1 cup Greek yoghurt (240g), 1 tablespoon honey (15g), 1 cup water (240ml)

UK: 75g raspberries (1/2 cup), 5g raspberry ketone powder (1 teaspoon), 240g Greek yoghurt (1 cup), 15g honey (1 tablespoon), 240ml water

Instructions:
Add the raspberries, raspberry ketone powder, Greek yoghurt, honey, and water to your Nutribullet. Blend on the 'Extract' setting until smooth.

Serve immediately in two glasses for a ketone boost.

Nutritional Info: Calories: 150 Fat: 4g Carbs: 22g Protein: 9g

CUCUMBER MINT HYDRATION HELPER

Prep: 5 mins Cook: N/A Serves: 2
Blending function used: Extract

Ingredients:

US: 1 cucumber (150g), 10 mint leaves (5g), 1/2 lemon (juiced), 1 cup coconut water (240ml), 1 teaspoon honey (5g)

UK: 150g cucumber (1), 5g mint leaves (10 leaves), 1/2 lemon (juiced), 240ml coconut water, 5g honey (1 teaspoon)

Instructions:

Place the cucumber, mint leaves, lemon juice, coconut water, and honey into the Nutribullet. Blend on the 'Extract' setting until smooth.

Pour into two glasses and enjoy your refreshing hydration helper immediately.

Nutritional Info: Calories: 45 Fat: 0g Carbs: 12g Protein: 0g

CHAPTER 5: HEART HEALTH HEROES

OATMEAL BERRY HEART HELPER

Prep: 5 mins Cook: 5 mins Serves: 1
Blending function used: Extract

Ingredients:

US: 60g rolled oats, 250ml almond milk, 100g mixed berries (blueberries, strawberries, raspberries), 1 tablespoon chia seeds, 1 tablespoon honey, 1 teaspoon ground flaxseed
UK: 60g rolled oats, 250ml almond milk, 100g mixed berries (blueberries, strawberries, raspberries), 1 tablespoon chia seeds, 1 tablespoon honey, 1 teaspoon ground flaxseed

Instructions:

Add the rolled oats and almond milk to your Nutribullet cup.
Top with mixed berries, chia seeds, honey, and ground flaxseed.
Secure the blade and blend using the Extract function until smooth.
Pour into a bowl and enjoy immediately for a heart-healthy start to your day!

Nutritional Info: Calories: 280 Fat: 8g Carbs: 46g Protein: 6g

SPINACH AVOCADO CHOLESTEROL BUSTER

Prep: 5 mins Cook: 0 mins Serves: 1
Blending function used: Blend

Ingredients:

US: 1 ripe avocado, 2 cups spinach, 250ml water, 1 tablespoon lemon juice, 1 tablespoon flaxseed oil, 1 apple (cored and chopped)
UK: 1 ripe avocado, 2 cups spinach, 250ml water, 1 tablespoon lemon juice, 1 tablespoon flaxseed oil, 1 apple (cored and chopped)

Instructions:

Scoop the avocado flesh into your Nutribullet cup.
Add the spinach, water, lemon juice, flaxseed oil, and chopped apple.
Blend until smooth using the Blend function.
Pour into a glass and drink immediately for a cholesterol-lowering boost!

Nutritional Info: Calories: 350 Fat: 25g Carbs: 30g Protein: 4g

BEET AND POMEGRANATE PRESSURE REDUCER

Prep: 10 mins Cook: 0 mins Serves: 1
Blending function used: Blend
Ingredients:
US: 1 medium beet (peeled and chopped), 1 cup pomegranate seeds, 1 small cucumber (chopped), 250ml water, 1 tablespoon lemon juice, 1 teaspoon honey
UK: 1 medium beet (peeled and chopped), 1 cup pomegranate seeds, 1 small cucumber (chopped), 250ml water, 1 tablespoon lemon juice, 1 teaspoon honey
Instructions:
Place the chopped beet, pomegranate seeds, and cucumber into your Nutribullet cup.
Add water, lemon juice, and honey.
Blend until smooth using the Blend function.
Pour into a glass and enjoy immediately to help lower your blood pressure!
Nutritional Info: Calories: 150 Fat: 1g Carbs: 36g Protein: 3g

OMEGA3 RICH FLAX AND CHIA BLEND

Prep: 5 mins Cook: 0 mins Serves: 1
Blending function used: Extract
Ingredients:
US: 1 tablespoon chia seeds, 1 tablespoon flaxseeds, 1 cup spinach, 1 banana, 250ml almond milk
UK: 1 tablespoon chia seeds, 1 tablespoon flaxseeds, 1 cup spinach, 1 banana, 250ml almond milk
Instructions:
Add chia seeds, flaxseeds, spinach, and bananas to your Nutribullet cup.
Pour in the almond milk.
Blend using the Extract function until smooth.
Drink immediately to boost your omega-3 intake!
Nutritional Info: Calories: 270 Fat: 12g Carbs: 34g Protein: 8g

GREEN TEA AND BERRIES ARTERY CLEANER

Prep: 5 mins Cook: 0 mins Serves: 1
Blending function used: Blend

Ingredients:

US: 1 cup brewed green tea (cooled), 1 cup mixed berries (blueberries, strawberries, raspberries), 1 tablespoon honey, 1 tablespoon lemon juice

UK: 1 cup brewed green tea (cooled), 1 cup mixed berries (blueberries, strawberries, raspberries), 1 tablespoon honey, 1 tablespoon lemon juice

Instructions:

Brew the green tea and let it cool.
Add the cooled green tea, mixed berries, honey, and lemon juice to your Nutribullet cup.
Blend until smooth using the Blend function.
Pour into a glass and enjoy immediately to help clean your arteries!

Nutritional Info: Calories: 120 Fat: 1g Carbs: 30g Protein: 1g

BANANA WALNUT POTASSIUM BOOSTER

Prep: 5 mins Cook: 0 mins Serves: 1
Blending function used: Extract

Ingredients:

US: 1 banana, 30g walnuts, 250ml almond milk, 1 tablespoon honey, 1 teaspoon vanilla extract
UK: 1 banana, 30g walnuts, 250ml almond milk, 1 tablespoon honey, 1 teaspoon vanilla extract

Instructions:

Peel the banana and place it in your Nutribullet cup.
Add the walnuts, almond milk, honey, and vanilla extract.
Blend using the Extract function until smooth.
Pour into a glass and drink immediately to boost your potassium levels!

Nutritional Info: Calories: 300 Fat: 15g Carbs: 40g Protein: 6g

KALE AND PINEAPPLE INFLAMMATION FIGHTER

Prep: 5 mins Cook: 0 mins Serves: 1

Blending function used: Blend

Ingredients:

US: 1 cup kale (stems removed), 1 cup pineapple chunks, 250ml coconut water, 1 tablespoon chia seeds

UK: 1 cup kale (stems removed), 1 cup pineapple chunks, 250ml coconut water, 1 tablespoon chia seeds

Instructions:

Remove the stems from the kale and add to your Nutribullet cup.

Add the pineapple chunks, coconut water, and chia seeds.

Blend until smooth using the Blend function.

Pour into a glass and enjoy immediately to fight inflammation!

Nutritional Info: Calories: 180 Fat: 4g Carbs: 36g Protein: 4g

COCOA AND ALMOND HEART PROTECTOR

Prep: 5 mins Cook: 0 mins Serves: 1

Blending function used: Extract

Ingredients:

US: 1 tablespoon cocoa powder, 30g almonds, 1 banana, 250ml almond milk, 1 tablespoon honey

UK: 1 tablespoon cocoa powder, 30g almonds, 1 banana, 250ml almond milk, 1 tablespoon honey

Instructions:

Add the cocoa powder, almonds, banana, almond milk, and honey to your Nutribullet cup.

Blend using the Extract function until smooth.

Pour into a glass and enjoy immediately to protect your heart!

Nutritional Info: Calories: 350 Fat: 18g Carbs: 40g Protein: 10g

TOMATO LYCOPENE HEART SHIELD

Prep: 5 mins Cook: 0 mins Serves: 1

Blending function used: Blend

Ingredients:

US: 2 ripe tomatoes (chopped), 1 small carrot (peeled and chopped), 1 stalk celery (chopped), 250ml water, 1 tablespoon lemon juice

UK: 2 ripe tomatoes (chopped), 1 small carrot (peeled and chopped), 1 stalk celery (chopped), 250ml water, 1 tablespoon lemon juice

Instructions:

Chop the tomatoes, carrots, and celery and add to your Nutribullet cup.
Add water and lemon juice.
Blend until smooth using the Blend function.
Pour into a glass and enjoy immediately to shield your heart with lycopene!

Nutritional Info: Calories: 90 Fat: 1g Carbs: 21g Protein: 2g

WATERMELON CITRULLINE CARDIO BOOSTER

Prep: 5 mins Cook: 0 mins Serves: 1

Blending function used: Blend

Ingredients:

US: 2 cups watermelon chunks, 1 small cucumber (chopped), 1 tablespoon lime juice, 1 teaspoon honey

UK: 2 cups watermelon chunks, 1 small cucumber (chopped), 1 tablespoon lime juice, 1 teaspoon honey

Instructions:

Add the watermelon chunks and chopped cucumber to your Nutribullet cup.
Add lime juice and honey.
Blend until smooth using the Blend function.
Pour into a glass and enjoy immediately to boost your cardiovascular health with citrulline!

Nutritional Info: Calories: 100 Fat: 0g Carbs: 26g Protein: 1g

GRAPE AND RESVERATROL HEART TONIC

Prep: 5 mins Cook: 0 mins Serves: 1

Blending function used: Extract

Ingredients:

US: 1 cup red grapes, 1 small apple (cored and chopped), 1 tablespoon lemon juice, 250ml water, 1 teaspoon honey

UK: 1 cup red grapes, 1 small apple (cored and chopped), 1 tablespoon lemon juice, 250ml water, 1 teaspoon honey

Instructions:

Place the red grapes and chopped apple into your Nutribullet cup.

Add the lemon juice, water, and honey.

Blend using the Extract function until smooth.

Pour into a glass and drink immediately to benefit from the heartprotective resveratrol!

Nutritional Info: Calories: 150 Fat: 0g Carbs: 38g Protein: 1g

GINGER TURMERIC CIRCULATION ENHANCER

Prep: 5 mins Cook: 0 mins Serves: 1

Blending function used: Blend

Ingredients:

US: 1 small piece of ginger (peeled), 1 teaspoon turmeric powder, 1 cup carrot juice, 1 cup orange juice, 1 teaspoon honey

UK: 1 small piece of ginger (peeled), 1 teaspoon turmeric powder, 1 cup carrot juice, 1 cup orange juice, 1 teaspoon honey

Instructions:

Peel the ginger and add it to your Nutribullet cup.

Add the turmeric powder, carrot juice, orange juice, and honey.

Blend using the Blend function until well mixed.

Pour into a glass and enjoy immediately to enhance your circulation with the power of ginger and turmeric!

Nutritional Info: Calories: 120 Fat: 0g Carbs: 30g Protein: 2g

BLUEBERRY OAT FIBER BOOSTER

Prep: 5 mins Cook: 0 mins Serves: 1

Blending function used: Extract

Ingredients:

US: 1 cup blueberries, 1/2 cup rolled oats, 250ml almond milk, 1 tablespoon chia seeds, 1 tablespoon honey

UK: 1 cup blueberries, 1/2 cup rolled oats, 250ml almond milk, 1 tablespoon chia seeds, 1 tablespoon honey

Instructions:

Add the blueberries, rolled oats, and chia seeds to your Nutribullet cup.

Pour in the almond milk and honey.

Blend using the Extract function until smooth.

Pour into a glass and drink immediately to boost fibre intake and support heart health!

Nutritional Info: Calories: 250 Fat: 7g Carbs: 43g Protein: 6g

CHAPTER 6: ENERGY BOOSTERS

Espresso Protein Punch

Prep: 5 mins Cook: 0 mins Serves: 1

Blending function used: Extract

Ingredients:

US: 1 shot espresso (30ml), 250ml almond milk, 1 banana, 1 tablespoon almond butter, 1 tablespoon honey, 1 scoop protein powder

UK: 1 shot espresso (30ml), 250ml almond milk, 1 banana, 1 tablespoon almond butter, 1 tablespoon honey, 1 scoop protein powder

Instructions:

Brew a shot of espresso and let it cool slightly.

Add the espresso, almond milk, banana, almond butter, honey, and protein powder to your Nutribullet cup.

Secure the blade and blend using the Extract function until smooth.

Pour into a glass and enjoy immediately for a delicious and energising protein punch!

Nutritional Info: Calories: 350 Fat: 14g Carbs: 40g Protein: 20g

GREEN TEA ENERGISER

Prep: 5 mins Cook: 0 mins Serves: 1
Blending function used: Blend

Ingredients:

US: 1 cup brewed green tea (cooled), 1 cup spinach, 1 banana, 1 tablespoon honey, 1 teaspoon chia seeds

UK: 1 cup brewed green tea (cooled), 1 cup spinach, 1 banana, 1 tablespoon honey, 1 teaspoon chia seeds

Instructions:

Brew a cup of green tea and let it cool.
Add the cooled green tea, spinach, banana, honey, and chia seeds to your Nutribullet cup.
Blend using the Blend function until smooth.
Pour into a glass and enjoy immediately for a refreshing energy boost!

Nutritional Info: Calories: 180 Fat: 2g Carbs: 42g Protein: 3g

BEETROOT PREWORKOUT BOOSTER

Prep: 10 mins Cook: 0 mins Serves: 1
Blending function used: Blend

Ingredients:

US: 1 small beetroot (peeled and chopped), 1 apple (cored and chopped), 1 small carrot (peeled and chopped), 250ml water, 1 tablespoon lemon juice

UK: 1 small beetroot (peeled and chopped), 1 apple (cored and chopped), 1 small carrot (peeled and chopped), 250ml water, 1 tablespoon lemon juice

Instructions:

Peel and chop the beetroot, apple, and carrot, then add them to your Nutribullet cup.
Add the water and lemon juice.
Blend using the Blend function until smooth.
Pour into a glass and enjoy immediately to fuel your workout with natural energy!

Nutritional Info: Calories: 150 Fat: 0g Carbs: 38g Protein: 2g

BANANA OAT ENERGY BLAST

Prep: 5 mins Cook: 0 mins Serves: 1
Blending function used: Extract
Ingredients:
US: 1 banana, 50g rolled oats, 250ml almond milk, 1 tablespoon honey, 1 teaspoon cinnamon
UK: 1 banana, 50g rolled oats, 250ml almond milk, 1 tablespoon honey, 1 teaspoon cinnamon
Instructions:
Peel the banana and place it in your Nutribullet cup.
Add the rolled oats, almond milk, honey, and cinnamon.
Blend using the Extract function until smooth.
Pour into a glass and drink immediately for a sustained energy boost!
Nutritional Info: Calories: 280 Fat: 5g Carbs: 54g Protein: 6g

MACA ROOT POWERUP

Prep: 5 mins Cook: 0 mins Serves: 1
Blending function used: Blend
Ingredients:
US: 1 tablespoon maca powder, 1 cup almond milk, 1 banana, 1 tablespoon almond butter, 1 teaspoon honey
UK: 1 tablespoon maca powder, 1 cup almond milk, 1 banana, 1 tablespoon almond butter, 1 teaspoon honey
Instructions:
Add the maca powder, almond milk, banana, almond butter, and honey to your Nutribullet cup.
Blend using the Blend function until smooth.
Pour into a glass and enjoy immediately to power up your day with natural energy!
Nutritional Info: Calories: 300 Fat: 14g Carbs: 39g Protein: 7g

GINSENG GINGER ZING

Prep: 5 mins Cook: 0 mins Serves: 1
Blending function used: Blend
Ingredients:
US: 1 small piece of ginger (peeled), 1 teaspoon ginseng powder, 1 cup orange juice, 1 tablespoon honey
UK: 1 small piece of ginger (peeled), 1 teaspoon ginseng powder, 1 cup orange juice, 1 tablespoon honey
Instructions:
Peel the ginger and add it to your Nutribullet cup.
Add the ginseng powder, orange juice, and honey.
Blend using the Blend function until smooth.
Pour into a glass and enjoy immediately for a zingy energy boost!
Nutritional Info: Calories: 120 Fat: 0g Carbs: 31g Protein: 1g

COCONUT WATER ELECTROLYTE REPLENISHER

Prep: 5 mins Cook: 0 mins Serves: 1
Blending function used: Blend
Ingredients:
US: 250ml coconut water, 1 banana, 1 cup pineapple chunks, 1 tablespoon honey
UK: 250ml coconut water, 1 banana, 1 cup pineapple chunks, 1 tablespoon honey
Instructions:
Add the coconut water, banana, pineapple chunks, and honey to your Nutribullet cup.
Blend using the Blend function until smooth.
Pour into a glass and drink immediately to replenish your electrolytes and rehydrate!
Nutritional Info: Calories: 200 Fat: 0g Carbs: 52g Protein: 2g

CACAO NIB ENERGY BITES SMOOTHIE

Prep: 5 mins Cook: 0 mins Serves: 1

Blending function used: Extract

Ingredients:

US: 1 tablespoon cacao nibs, 1 banana, 250ml almond milk, 1 tablespoon almond butter, 1 tablespoon honey

UK: 1 tablespoon cacao nibs, 1 banana, 250ml almond milk, 1 tablespoon almond butter, 1 tablespoon honey

Instructions:

Add the cacao nibs, banana, almond milk, butter, and honey to your Nutribullet cup.

Blend using the Extract function until smooth.

Pour into a glass and enjoy immediately for a tasty and energising treat!

Nutritional Info: Calories: 350 Fat: 18g Carbs: 42g Protein: 8g

SPIRULINA SUPERFOOD ENERGISER

Prep: 5 mins Cook: 0 mins Serves: 1

Blending function used: Blend

Ingredients:

US: 1 teaspoon spirulina powder, 1 cup spinach, 1 banana, 250ml coconut water, 1 tablespoon honey

UK: 1 teaspoon spirulina powder, 1 cup spinach, 1 banana, 250ml coconut water, 1 tablespoon honey

Instructions:

Add the spirulina powder, spinach, banana, coconut water, and honey to your Nutribullet cup.

Blend using the Blend function until smooth.

Pour into a glass and enjoy immediately for a superfood energy boost!

Nutritional Info: Calories: 220 Fat: 1g Carbs: 55g Protein: 3g

MATCHA GREEN TEA FOCUSER

Prep: 5 mins Cook: 0 mins Serves: 1
Blending function used: Blend

Ingredients:

US: 1 teaspoon matcha powder, 1 cup almond milk, 1 banana, 1 tablespoon honey
UK: 1 teaspoon matcha powder, 1 cup almond milk, 1 banana, 1 tablespoon honey

Instructions:

Add the matcha powder, almond milk, banana, and honey to your Nutribullet cup.
Blend using the Blend function until smooth.
Pour into a glass and enjoy immediately to stay focused and energised!

Nutritional Info: Calories: 250 Fat: 5g Carbs: 47g Protein: 5g

CHIA SEED SUSTAINER

Prep: 5 mins Cook: 0 mins Serves: 1
Blending function used: Extract

Ingredients:

US: 1 tablespoon chia seeds, 1 cup almond milk, 1 banana, 1 tablespoon honey, 1/2 teaspoon vanilla extract

UK: 1 tablespoon chia seeds, 1 cup almond milk, 1 banana, 1 tablespoon honey, 1/2 teaspoon vanilla extract

Instructions:

Add the chia seeds, almond milk, banana, honey, and vanilla extract to your Nutribullet cup. Blend using the Extract function until smooth.

Pour into a glass and enjoy immediately for sustained energy and satiety!

Nutritional Info: Calories: 220 Fat: 6g Carbs: 38g Protein: 4g

BVITAMIN BOOST BLEND

Prep: 5 mins Cook: 0 mins Serves: 1
Blending function used: Blend

Ingredients:

US: 1 cup spinach, 1/2 avocado, 1 banana, 1 cup orange juice, 1 tablespoon honey
UK: 1 cup spinach, 1/2 avocado, 1 banana, 1 cup orange juice, 1 tablespoon honey

Instructions:

Add the spinach, avocado, banana, orange juice, and honey to your Nutribullet cup. Blend using the Blend function until smooth.

Pour into a glass and enjoy immediately for a boost of B vitamins to energise your day!

Nutritional Info: Calories: 240 Fat: 9g Carbs: 38g Protein: 4g

GUARANA BERRY ENERGY KICK

Prep: 5 mins Cook: 0 mins Serves: 1

Blending function used: Extract

Ingredients:

US: 1 teaspoon guarana powder, 1 cup mixed berries, 1 banana, 1 cup coconut water, 1 tablespoon honey

UK: 1 teaspoon guarana powder, 1 cup mixed berries, 1 banana, 1 cup coconut water, 1 tablespoon honey

Instructions:

Add the guarana powder, mixed berries, banana, coconut water, and honey to your Nutribullet cup. Blend using the Extract function until smooth.

Pour into a glass and enjoy immediately for a natural energy kick!

Nutritional Info: Calories: 180 Fat: 1g Carbs: 46g Protein: 2g

CHAPTER 7: SUPERFOOD SENSATIONS

ACAI BERRY BOWL BLEND

Prep: 10 mins Cook: 0 mins Serves: 1
Blending function used: Extract

Ingredients:

US: 100g frozen acai puree, 1 banana, 100g mixed berries, 100ml almond milk, 1 tablespoon honey
UK: 100g frozen acai puree, 1 banana, 100g mixed berries, 100ml almond milk, 1 tablespoon honey

Instructions:

Add the acai puree, banana, mixed berries, almond milk, and honey to your Nutribullet cup.
Blend using the Extract function until smooth.
Pour into a bowl and top with your favourite toppings like granola, fresh fruit, and coconut flakes.
Enjoy immediately for a refreshing and antioxidant-packed breakfast bowl!

Nutritional Info: Calories: 250 Fat: 3g Carbs: 55g Protein: 3g

GOJI BERRY ANTIOXIDANT BLAST

Prep: 10 mins Cook: 0 mins Serves: 1
Blending function used: Extract

Ingredients:

US: 30g goji berries, 1 cup mixed berries, 1 banana, 200ml coconut water, 1 tablespoon honey
UK: 30g goji berries, 1 cup mixed berries, 1 banana, 200ml coconut water, 1 tablespoon honey

Instructions:

Add goji, mixed berries, banana, coconut water, and honey to your Nutribullet cup.
Blend using the Extract function until smooth.
Pour into a glass and enjoy immediately for a powerful antioxidant boost!

Nutritional Info: Calories: 220 Fat: 1g Carbs: 54g Protein: 2g

SPIRULINA GREEN GODDESS

Prep: 10 mins Cook: 0 mins Serves: 1
Blending function used: Blend
Ingredients:
US: 1 teaspoon spirulina powder, 1 cup spinach, 1 banana, 1/2 avocado, 200ml coconut water, 1 tablespoon honey
UK: 1 teaspoon spirulina powder, 1 cup spinach, 1 banana, 1/2 avocado, 200ml coconut water, 1 tablespoon honey
Instructions:
Add the spirulina powder, spinach, banana, avocado, coconut water, and honey to your Nutribullet cup.
Blend using the Blend function until smooth.
Pour into a glass and enjoy immediately for a nutrient-rich green smoothie!
Nutritional Info: Calories: 250 Fat: 10g Carbs: 38g Protein: 4g

MACA ROOT HORMONE BALANCER

Prep: 5 mins Cook: 0 mins Serves: 1
Blending function used: Blend
Ingredients:
US: 1 teaspoon maca powder, 1 cup almond milk, 1 banana, 1 tablespoon almond butter, 1 tablespoon honey
UK: 1 teaspoon maca powder, 1 cup almond milk, 1 banana, 1 tablespoon almond butter, 1 tablespoon honey
Instructions:
Add the maca powder, almond milk, banana, almond butter, and honey to your Nutribullet cup.
Blend using the Blend function until smooth.
Pour into a glass and enjoy immediately for a natural hormone balance!
Nutritional Info: Calories: 280 Fat: 12g Carbs: 40g Protein: 6g

CACAO NIB MOOD LIFTER

Prep: 5 mins Cook: 0 mins Serves: 1
Blending function used: Blend

Ingredients:

US: 1 tablespoon cacao nibs, 1 banana, 1 cup almond milk, 1 tablespoon honey, 1 teaspoon vanilla extract

UK: 1 tablespoon cacao nibs, 1 banana, 1 cup almond milk, 1 tablespoon honey, 1 teaspoon vanilla extract

Instructions:

Add the cacao nibs, banana, almond milk, honey, and vanilla extract to your Nutribullet cup.
Blend using the Blend function until smooth.
Pour into a glass and enjoy immediately for a mood-boosting treat!

Nutritional Info: Calories: 250 Fat: 8g Carbs: 42g Protein: 5g

CHIA SEED OMEGA BOOSTER

Prep: 5 mins Cook: 0 mins Serves: 1
Blending function used: Extract

Ingredients:

US: 1 tablespoon chia seeds, 1 cup almond milk, 1 banana, 1/2 cup blueberries, 1 tablespoon honey
UK: 1 tablespoon chia seeds, 1 cup almond milk, 1 banana, 1/2 cup blueberries, 1 tablespoon honey

Instructions:

Add the chia seeds, almond milk, banana, blueberries, and honey to your Nutribullet cup.
Blend using the Extract function until smooth.
Pour into a glass and enjoy immediately for a boost of omega-3 fatty acids!

Nutritional Info: Calories: 220 Fat: 6g Carbs: 38g Protein: 4g

HEMP PROTEIN POWERUP

Prep: 5 mins Cook: 0 mins Serves: 1
Blending function used: Blend
Ingredients:
US: 1 scoop hemp protein powder, 1 banana, 1 cup almond milk, 1 tablespoon honey, 1 teaspoon cinnamon
UK: 1 scoop hemp protein powder, 1 banana, 1 cup almond milk, 1 tablespoon honey, 1 teaspoon cinnamon
Instructions:
Add the hemp protein powder, banana, almond milk, honey, and cinnamon to your Nutribullet cup. Blend using the Blend function until smooth.
Pour into a glass and enjoy immediately for a protein-packed boost!
Nutritional Info: Calories: 250 Fat: 8g Carbs: 38g Protein: 15g

MORINGA LEAF NUTRIENTPACKED SMOOTHIE

Prep: 5 mins Cook: 0 mins Serves: 1
Blending function used: Extract
Ingredients:
US: 1 teaspoon moringa leaf powder, 1 cup spinach, 1 banana, 1 cup coconut water, 1 tablespoon honey
UK: 1 teaspoon moringa leaf powder, 1 cup spinach, 1 banana, 1 cup coconut water, 1 tablespoon honey
Instructions:
Add the moringa leaf powder, spinach, banana, coconut water, and honey to your Nutribullet cup. Blend using the Extract function until smooth.
Pour into a glass and enjoy immediately for a nutrient-dense smoothie!
Nutritional Info: Calories: 210 Fat: 1g Carbs: 50g Protein: 3g

TURMERIC GOLDEN MILK BLEND

Prep: 5 mins Cook: 0 mins Serves: 1
Blending function used: Blend

Ingredients:

US: 1 teaspoon turmeric powder, 1 cup almond milk, 1 banana, 1 tablespoon honey, 1/2 teaspoon cinnamon

UK: 1 teaspoon turmeric powder, 1 cup almond milk, 1 banana, 1 tablespoon honey, 1/2 teaspoon cinnamon

Instructions:

Add the turmeric powder, almond milk, banana, honey, and cinnamon to your Nutribullet cup.

Blend using the Blend function until smooth.

Pour into a glass and enjoy immediately for a soothing and anti-inflammatory drink!

Nutritional Info: Calories: 220 Fat: 4g Carbs: 45g Protein: 3g

WHEATGRASS SHOT SMOOTHER

Prep: 5 mins Cook: 0 mins Serves: 1
Blending function used: Blend

Ingredients:

US: 1 tablespoon wheatgrass powder, 1 cup pineapple chunks, 1 banana, 1 cup coconut water, 1 tablespoon honey

UK: 1 tablespoon wheatgrass powder, 1 cup pineapple chunks, 1 banana, 1 cup coconut water, 1 tablespoon honey

Instructions:

Add the wheatgrass powder, pineapple chunks, banana, coconut water, and honey to your Nutribullet cup.

Blend using the Blend function until smooth.

Pour into a glass and enjoy immediately for a quick and energising wheatgrass shot!

Nutritional Info: Calories: 230 Fat: 1g Carbs: 55g Protein: 2g

MATCHA GREEN TEA ANTIOXIDANT ELIXIR

Prep: 5 mins Cook: 0 mins Serves: 1

Blending function used: Blend

Ingredients:

US: 1 teaspoon matcha powder, 1 cup almond milk, 1 banana, 1 tablespoon honey, 1/2 teaspoon vanilla extract

UK: 1 teaspoon matcha powder, 1 cup almond milk, 1 banana, 1 tablespoon honey, 1/2 teaspoon vanilla extract

Instructions:

Add the matcha powder, almond milk, banana, honey, and vanilla extract to your Nutribullet cup. Blend using the Blend function until smooth.

Pour into a glass and enjoy immediately for an antioxidant-rich energy boost!

Nutritional Info: Calories: 220 Fat: 6g Carbs: 38g Protein: 4g

CHLORELLA CLEANSE AND ENERGIES

Prep: 5 mins Cook: 0 mins Serves: 1

Blending function used: Extract

Ingredients:

US: 1 teaspoon chlorella powder, 1 cup spinach, 1 banana, 200ml coconut water, 1 tablespoon honey
UK: 1 teaspoon chlorella powder, 1 cup spinach, 1 banana, 200ml coconut water, 1 tablespoon honey

Instructions:

Add the chlorella powder, spinach, banana, coconut water, and honey to your Nutribullet cup.
Blend using the Extract function until smooth.
Pour into a glass and enjoy immediately for a cleansing and energising drink!

Nutritional Info: Calories: 210 Fat: 1g Carbs: 50g Protein: 3g

BEE POLLEN IMMUNITY BOOSTER

Prep: 5 mins Cook: 0 mins Serves: 1

Blending function used: Extract

Ingredients:

US: 1 teaspoon bee pollen, 1 cup mixed berries, 1 banana, 200ml almond milk, 1 tablespoon honey
UK: 1 teaspoon bee pollen, 1 cup mixed berries, 1 banana, 200ml almond milk, 1 tablespoon honey

Instructions:

Add the bee pollen, mixed berries, banana, almond milk, and honey to your Nutribullet cup.
Blend using the Extract function until smooth.
Pour into a glass and enjoy immediately to boost your immune system!

Nutritional Info: Calories: 220 Fat: 3g Carbs: 46g Protein: 4g

CHAPTER 8: SEASONAL SMOOTHIE SPECIALTIES

SUMMER BERRY BLAST

Prep: 10 mins Cook: 0 mins Serves: 1

Blending function used: Extract

Ingredients:

US: 100g mixed berries (fresh or frozen), 1 banana, 200ml almond milk, 1 tablespoon honey, 1 teaspoon chia seeds

UK: 100g mixed berries (fresh or frozen), 1 banana, 200ml almond milk, 1 tablespoon honey, 1 teaspoon chia seeds

Instructions:

Add the mixed berries, banana, almond milk, honey, and chia seeds to your Nutribullet cup.

Blend using the Extract function until smooth.

Pour into a glass and enjoy immediately for a refreshing, berry-filled boost!

Nutritional Info: Calories: 230 Fat: 4g Carbs: 45g Protein: 4g

AUTUMN PUMPKIN SPICE SMOOTHIE

Prep: 10 mins Cook: 0 mins Serves: 1

Blending function used: Blend

Ingredients:

US: 1/2 cup canned pumpkin, 1 banana, 200ml almond milk, 1 teaspoon pumpkin spice, 1 tablespoon maple syrup

UK: 1/2 cup canned pumpkin, 1 banana, 200ml almond milk, 1 teaspoon pumpkin spice, 1 tablespoon maple syrup

Instructions:

Add the canned pumpkin, banana, almond milk, pumpkin spice, and maple syrup to your Nutribullet cup.

Blend using the Blend function until smooth.

Pour into a glass and enjoy immediately for a comforting autumn treat!

Nutritional Info: Calories: 270 Fat: 5g Carbs: 50g Protein: 4g

WINTER CITRUS IMMUNE BOOSTER

Prep: 10 mins Cook: 0 mins Serves: 1
Blending function used: Extract
Ingredients:
US: 1 orange, 1/2 lemon, 1 tablespoon fresh ginger, 1 tablespoon honey, 200ml water
UK: 1 orange, 1/2 lemon, 1 tablespoon fresh ginger, 1 tablespoon honey, 200ml water
Instructions:
Peel the orange and lemon, then add to your Nutribullet cup with fresh ginger, honey, and water.
Blend using the Extract function until smooth.
Pour into a glass and enjoy immediately to boost your immune system during winter!
Nutritional Info: Calories: 180 Fat: 0g Carbs: 45g Protein: 1g

SPRING GREENS RENEWAL BLEND

Prep: 10 mins Cook: 0 mins Serves: 1
Blending function used: Extract
Ingredients:
US: 1 cup spinach, 1/2 cucumber, 1 green apple, 200ml coconut water, 1 tablespoon lemon juice
UK: 1 cup spinach, 1/2 cucumber, 1 green apple, 200ml coconut water, 1 tablespoon lemon juice
Instructions:
Add the spinach, cucumber, green apple, coconut water, and lemon juice to your Nutribullet cup.
Blend using the Extract function until smooth.
Pour into a glass and enjoy immediately for a refreshing spring green smoothie!
Nutritional Info: Calories: 190 Fat: 1g Carbs: 45g Protein: 3g

WATERMELON COOLER

Prep: 10 mins Cook: 0 mins Serves: 1
Blending function used: Extract
Ingredients:
US: 200g watermelon, 1/2 lime, 1 tablespoon mint leaves, 1 tablespoon honey, 200ml water
UK: 200g watermelon, 1/2 lime, 1 tablespoon mint leaves, 1 tablespoon honey, 200ml water
Instructions:
Add the watermelon, lime, mint leaves, honey, and water to your Nutribullet cup.
Blend using the Extract function until smooth.
Pour into a glass and enjoy immediately for a cool, hydrating drink!
Nutritional Info: Calories: 160 Fat: 0g Carbs: 40g Protein: 1g

APPLE PIE SMOOTHIE

Prep: 10 mins Cook: 0 mins Serves: 1
Blending function used: Blend
Ingredients:
US: 1 apple, 1/2 teaspoon cinnamon, 1 cup almond milk, 1 banana, 1 tablespoon honey
UK: 1 apple, 1/2 teaspoon cinnamon, 1 cup almond milk, 1 banana, 1 tablespoon honey
Instructions:
Add the apple, cinnamon, almond milk, banana, and honey to your Nutribullet cup.
Blend using the Blend function until smooth.
Pour into a glass and enjoy immediately for a delicious, apple pie flavoured smoothie!
Nutritional Info: Calories: 250 Fat: 4g Carbs: 50g Protein: 3g

CRANBERRY ORANGE WINTER TONIC

Prep: 10 mins Cook: 0 mins Serves: 1

Blending function used: Extract

Ingredients:

US: 100g cranberries (fresh or frozen), 1 orange, 1 tablespoon honey, 200ml water
UK: 100g cranberries (fresh or frozen), 1 orange, 1 tablespoon honey, 200ml water

Instructions:

Add the cranberries, orange, honey, and water to your Nutribullet cup.
Blend using the Extract function until smooth.
Pour into a glass and enjoy immediately for a refreshing winter tonic!

Nutritional Info: Calories: 180 Fat: 0g Carbs: 45g Protein: 1g

ASPARAGUS AND PEA SPRING CLEANSE

Prep: 10 mins Cook: 0 mins Serves: 1

Blending function used: Extract

Ingredients:

US: 1/2 cup asparagus tips, 1/2 cup peas, 1 green apple, 200ml coconut water, 1 tablespoon lemon juice
UK: 1/2 cup asparagus tips, 1/2 cup peas, 1 green apple, 200ml coconut water, 1 tablespoon lemon juice

Instructions:

Add the asparagus tips, peas, green apple, coconut water, and lemon juice to your Nutribullet cup.
Blend using the Extract function until smooth.
Pour into a glass and enjoy immediately for a springtime cleanse!

Nutritional Info: Calories: 190 Fat: 1g Carbs: 45g Protein: 4g

PEACH MELBA SUMMER SLIMMER

Prep: 10 mins Cook: 0 mins Serves: 1
Blending function used: Extract
Ingredients:
US: 1 cup peaches (fresh or frozen), 1/2 cup raspberries, 200ml almond milk, 1 tablespoon honey
UK: 1 cup peaches (fresh or frozen), 1/2 cup raspberries, 200ml almond milk, 1 tablespoon honey
Instructions:
Add the peaches, raspberries, almond milk, and honey to your Nutribullet cup.
Blend using the Extract function until smooth.
Pour into a glass and enjoy immediately for a peachy, summer-slimming treat!
Nutritional Info: Calories: 230 Fat: 3g Carbs: 50g Protein: 3g

CINNAMON PERSIMMON FALL WARMER

Prep: 10 mins Cook: 0 mins Serves: 1
Blending function used: Blend
Ingredients:
US: 1 ripe persimmon, 1 banana, 1 cup almond milk, 1/2 teaspoon cinnamon, 1 tablespoon honey
UK: 1 ripe persimmon, 1 banana, 1 cup almond milk, 1/2 teaspoon cinnamon, 1 tablespoon honey
Instructions:
Add the persimmon, banana, almond milk, cinnamon, and honey to your Nutribullet cup.
Blend using the Blend function until smooth.
Pour into a glass and enjoy immediately for a warm, autumn-inspired smoothie!
Nutritional Info: Calories: 250 Fat: 4g Carbs: 52g Protein: 3g

GINGERBREAD COOKIE PROTEIN SHAKE

Prep: 10 mins Cook: 0 mins Serves: 1

Blending function used: Blend

Ingredients:

US: 1 scoop vanilla protein powder, 1/2 teaspoon ground ginger, 1/2 teaspoon ground cinnamon, 1 cup almond milk, 1 banana, 1 tablespoon molasses

UK: 1 scoop vanilla protein powder, 1/2 teaspoon ground ginger, 1/2 teaspoon ground cinnamon, 1 cup almond milk, 1 banana, 1 tablespoon molasses

Instructions:

Add the vanilla protein powder, ground ginger, ground cinnamon, almond milk, banana, and molasses to your Nutribullet cup.

Blend using the Blend function until smooth.

Pour into a glass and enjoy immediately for a protein-packed, gingerbread-flavoured treat!

Nutritional Info: Calories: 290 Fat: 5g Carbs: 45g Protein: 20g

STRAWBERRY RHUBARB SPRING TONIC

Prep: 10 mins Cook: 0 mins Serves: 1

Blending function used: Extract

Ingredients:

US: 100g strawberries (fresh or frozen), 100g rhubarb, 1 green apple, 200ml water, 1 tablespoon honey

UK: 100g strawberries (fresh or frozen), 100g rhubarb, 1 green apple, 200ml water, 1 tablespoon honey

Instructions:

Add the strawberries, rhubarb, green apple, water, and honey to your Nutribullet cup.
Blend using the Extract function until smooth.
Pour into a glass and enjoy immediately for a refreshing spring tonic with a tangy twist!

Nutritional Info: Calories: 180 Fat: 1g Carbs: 43g Protein: 2g

FIG AND HONEY AUTUMN BLEND

Prep: 10 mins Cook: 0 mins Serves: 1

Blending function used: Blend

Ingredients:

US: 5 fresh figs, 1 banana, 1 cup almond milk, 1 tablespoon honey, 1/2 teaspoon vanilla extract
UK: 5 fresh figs, 1 banana, 1 cup almond milk, 1 tablespoon honey, 1/2 teaspoon vanilla extract

Instructions:

Add the figs, banana, almond milk, honey, and vanilla extract to your Nutribullet cup.
Blend using the Blend function until smooth.
Pour into a glass and enjoy immediately for a sweet, figgy autumn delight!

Nutritional Info: Calories: 260 Fat: 4g Carbs: 55g Protein: 3g

CHAPTER 9: KIDFRIENDLY SMOOTHIES

BANANA SPLIT SMOOTHIE

Prep: 10 mins Cook: 0 mins Serves: 1

Blending function used: Blend

Ingredients:

US: 1 banana, 1/2 cup strawberries (fresh or frozen), 1/2 cup pineapple chunks, 1 cup vanilla yoghurt, 1 tablespoon honey

UK: 1 banana, 1/2 cup strawberries (fresh or frozen), 1/2 cup pineapple chunks, 1 cup vanilla yoghurt, 1 tablespoon honey

Instructions:

Add the banana, strawberries, pineapple chunks, vanilla yoghurt, and honey to your Nutribullet cup. Blend using the Blend function until smooth.

Pour into a glass and serve immediately for a fun, fruity treat!

Nutritional Info: Calories: 320 Fat: 6g Carbs: 65g Protein: 8g

HIDDEN VEGGIE BERRY BLAST

Prep: 10 mins Cook: 0 mins Serves: 1

Blending function used: Extract

Ingredients:

US: 1/2 cup spinach, 1/2 cup blueberries, 1/2 cup strawberries, 1/2 cup Greek yogurt, 1 tablespoon honey, 200ml water

UK: 1/2 cup spinach, 1/2 cup blueberries, 1/2 cup strawberries, 1/2 cup Greek yogurt, 1 tablespoon honey, 200ml water

Instructions:

Add the spinach, blueberries, strawberries, Greek yoghurt, honey, and water to your Nutribullet cup. Blend using the Extract function until smooth.

Pour into a glass and serve immediately for a smoothie packed with hidden veggies!

Nutritional Info: Calories: 250 Fat: 4g Carbs: 45g Protein: 12g

GREEN MONSTER SHAKE

Prep: 10 mins Cook: 0 mins Serves: 1

Blending function used: Extract

Ingredients:

US: 1/2 avocado, 1/2 cup spinach, 1 banana, 1/2 cup pineapple, 200ml coconut water

UK: 1/2 avocado, 1/2 cup spinach, 1 banana, 1/2 cup pineapple, 200ml coconut water

Instructions:

Add the avocado, spinach, banana, pineapple, and coconut water to your Nutribullet cup.

Blend using the Extract function until smooth.

Pour into a glass and serve immediately for a nutrientpacked shake!

Nutritional Info: Calories: 290 Fat: 15g Carbs: 35g Protein: 4g

PEANUT BUTTER AND JELLY SMOOTHIE

Prep: 10 mins Cook: 0 mins Serves: 1

Blending function used: Blend

Ingredients:

US: 1 tablespoon peanut butter, 1/2 cup strawberries, 1 banana, 1 cup almond milk, 1 tablespoon honey

UK: 1 tablespoon peanut butter, 1/2 cup strawberries, 1 banana, 1 cup almond milk, 1 tablespoon honey

Instructions:

Add the peanut butter, strawberries, banana, almond milk, and honey to your Nutribullet cup.

Blend using the Blend function until smooth.

Pour into a glass and serve immediately for a smoothie with a classic flavour!

Nutritional Info: Calories: 310 Fat: 12g Carbs: 45g Protein: 8g

CHOCOLATE CHIP COOKIE DOUGH SHAKE

Prep: 10 mins Cook: 0 mins Serves: 1
Blending function used: Blend

Ingredients:

US: 1 scoop chocolate protein powder, 1/4 cup oats, 1 tablespoon chocolate chips, 1 banana, 1 cup milk

UK: 1 scoop chocolate protein powder, 1/4 cup oats, 1 tablespoon chocolate chips, 1 banana, 1 cup milk

Instructions:

Add the chocolate protein powder, oats, chocolate chips, banana, and milk to your Nutribullet cup. Blend using the Blend function until smooth.

Pour into a glass and serve immediately for a shake that tastes like cookie dough!

Nutritional Info: Calories: 350 Fat: 9g Carbs: 50g Protein: 20g

RAINBOW FRUIT SMOOTHIE

Prep: 10 mins Cook: 0 mins Serves: 1
Blending function used: Extract

Ingredients:

US: 1/2 cup mango, 1/2 cup strawberries, 1/2 cup blueberries, 1 banana, 200ml orange juice
UK: 1/2 cup mango, 1/2 cup strawberries, 1/2 cup blueberries, 1 banana, 200ml orange juice

Instructions:

Add the mango, strawberries, blueberries, banana, and orange juice to your Nutribullet cup. Blend using the Extract function until smooth.

Pour into a glass and serve immediately for a vibrant, fruity smoothie!

Nutritional Info: Calories: 270 Fat: 1g Carbs: 60g Protein: 3g

CREAMSICLE DREAM

Prep: 10 mins Cook: 0 mins Serves: 1
Blending function used: Blend
Ingredients:
US: 1/2 cup orange juice, 1/2 cup vanilla yogurt, 1/2 banana, 1/2 cup ice, 1 tablespoon honey
UK: 1/2 cup orange juice, 1/2 cup vanilla yogurt, 1/2 banana, 1/2 cup ice, 1 tablespoon honey
Instructions:
Add the orange juice, vanilla yoghurt, banana, ice, and honey to your Nutribullet cup.
Blend using the Blend function until smooth.
Pour into a glass and serve immediately for a smoothie that tastes like a creamsicle!
Nutritional Info: Calories: 230 Fat: 3g Carbs: 45g Protein: 6g

APPLE PIE A LA MODE SMOOTHIE

Prep: 10 mins Cook: 0 mins Serves: 1
Blending function used: Blend
Ingredients:
US: 1 apple, 1/2 teaspoon cinnamon, 1/2 cup vanilla yogurt, 1/2 banana, 1 cup milk
UK: 1 apple, 1/2 teaspoon cinnamon, 1/2 cup vanilla yogurt, 1/2 banana, 1 cup milk
Instructions:
Add the apple, cinnamon, vanilla yoghurt, banana, and milk to your Nutribullet cup.
Blend using the Blend function until smooth.
Pour into a glass and serve immediately for a smoothie that tastes like apple pie!
Nutritional Info: Calories: 280 Fat: 6g Carbs: 50g Protein: 7g

WATERMELON SLUSHIE

Prep: 10 mins Cook: 0 mins Serves: 1
Blending function used: Extract

Ingredients:

US: 1 cup watermelon chunks, 1/2 lime (juiced), 1 tablespoon honey, 1/2 cup ice, 200ml water
UK: 1 cup watermelon chunks, 1/2 lime (juiced), 1 tablespoon honey, 1/2 cup ice, 200ml water

Instructions:

Add the watermelon chunks, lime juice, honey, ice, and water to your Nutribullet cup.
Blend using the Extract function until smooth.
Pour into a glass and serve immediately for a refreshing summer slushie!

Nutritional Info: Calories: 150 Fat: 0g Carbs: 37g Protein: 1g

STRAWBERRY MILK

Prep: 10 mins Cook: 0 mins Serves: 1
Blending function used: Blend

Ingredients:

US: 1 cup strawberries, 1 cup milk, 1 tablespoon honey, 1/2 teaspoon vanilla extract
UK: 1 cup strawberries, 1 cup milk, 1 tablespoon honey, 1/2 teaspoon vanilla extract

Instructions:

Add the strawberries, milk, honey, and vanilla extract to your Nutribullet cup.
Blend using the Blend function until smooth.
Pour into a glass and serve immediately for a delicious twist on classic milk!

Nutritional Info: Calories: 220 Fat: 6g Carbs: 35g Protein: 8g

TROPICAL COCONUT PINEAPPLE SMOOTHIE

Prep: 10 mins Cook: 0 mins Serves: 1

Blending function used: Extract

Ingredients:

US: 1 cup pineapple chunks, 1/2 cup coconut milk, 1 banana, 1/2 cup Greek yoghurt, 1 tablespoon honey

UK: 1 cup pineapple chunks, 1/2 cup coconut milk, 1 banana, 1/2 cup Greek yoghurt, 1 tablespoon honey

Instructions:

Add the pineapple chunks, coconut milk, banana, Greek yoghurt, and honey to your Nutribullet cup. Blend using the Extract function until smooth.

Pour into a glass and serve immediately for a creamy, tropical treat!

Nutritional Info: Calories: 280 Fat: 9g Carbs: 47g Protein: 7g

PURPLE POWER SMOOTHIE

Prep: 10 mins Cook: 0 mins Serves: 1
Blending function used: Extract

Ingredients:

US: 1/2 cup blueberries, 1/2 cup purple grapes, 1/2 cup Greek yogurt, 1 banana, 1/2 cup water
UK: 1/2 cup blueberries, 1/2 cup purple grapes, 1/2 cup Greek yogurt, 1 banana, 1/2 cup water

Instructions:

Add the blueberries, purple grapes, Greek yoghurt, banana, and water to your Nutribullet cup. Blend using the Extract function until smooth.

Pour into a glass and serve immediately for a vibrant, nutrientpacked smoothie!

Nutritional Info: Calories: 230 Fat: 2g Carbs: 50g Protein: 9g

NUTELLA BANANA SHAKE

Prep: 10 mins Cook: 0 mins Serves: 1
Blending function used: Blend

Ingredients:

US: 2 tablespoons Nutella, 1 banana, 1 cup milk, 1 tablespoon honey, 1/2 cup ice
UK: 2 tablespoons Nutella, 1 banana, 1 cup milk, 1 tablespoon honey, 1/2 cup ice

Instructions:

Add the Nutella, banana, milk, honey, and ice to your Nutribullet cup.
Blend using the Blend function until smooth.
Pour into a glass and serve immediately for a rich and creamy shake with a chocolatey twist!

Nutritional Info: Calories: 320 Fat: 13g Carbs: 45g Protein: 8g

CHAPTER 10: PROTEINPACKED POSTWORKOUT SMOOTHIES

CHOCOLATE BANANA PROTEIN SHAKE

Prep: 5 mins Cook: 0 mins Serves: 1 smoothie

Blending function used: Extract

Ingredients:

US: 1 medium banana, 240ml almond milk, 30g chocolate protein powder, 1 tablespoon peanut butter, 1 teaspoon cocoa powder, 5 ice cubes

UK: 1 medium banana, 240ml almond milk, 30g chocolate protein powder, 1 tablespoon peanut butter, 1 teaspoon cocoa powder, 5 ice cubes

Instructions:

Place the banana, almond milk, chocolate protein powder, peanut butter, cocoa powder, and ice cubes into your Nutribullet.

Secure the lid and blend on the Extract setting until smooth.

Pour into a glass and enjoy your delicious and proteinpacked shake!

Nutritional Info: Calories: 320 Fat: 12g Carbs: 40g Protein: 20g

VANILLA ALMOND MUSCLE BUILDER

Prep: 5 mins Cook: 0 mins Serves: 1 smoothie

Blending function used: Extract

Ingredients:

US: 240ml almond milk, 30g vanilla protein powder, 1 tablespoon almond butter, 1 teaspoon honey, 5 ice cubes

UK: 240ml almond milk, 30g vanilla protein powder, 1 tablespoon almond butter, 1 teaspoon honey, 5 ice cubes

Instructions:

Add almond milk, vanilla protein powder, almond butter, honey, and ice cubes to your Nutribullet.

Secure the lid and blend on the Extract setting until creamy.

Pour into a glass and savour your musclebuilding smoothie!

Nutritional Info: Calories: 290 Fat: 11g Carbs: 24g Protein: 22g

BERRY BLAST RECOVERY SMOOTHIE

Prep: 5 mins Cook: 0 mins Serves: 1 smoothie

Blending function used: Extract

Ingredients:

US: 150g mixed berries (frozen), 240ml coconut water, 30g berryflavored protein powder, 1 tablespoon chia seeds, 5 ice cubes

UK: 150g mixed berries (frozen), 240ml coconut water, 30g berryflavored protein powder, 1 tablespoon chia seeds, 5 ice cubes

Instructions:

Combine mixed berries, coconut water, berry protein powder, chia seeds, and ice cubes in your Nutribullet.

Secure the lid and blend on the Extract setting until smooth.

Pour into a glass and relish your refreshing recovery smoothie!

Nutritional Info: Calories: 200 Fat: 5g Carbs: 30g Protein: 15g

GREEN PROTEIN MACHINE

Prep: 5 mins Cook: 0 mins Serves: 1 smoothie

Blending function used: Extract

Ingredients:

US: 1 handful spinach, 1 medium apple (cored and chopped), 240ml water, 30g vanilla protein powder, 1 tablespoon flax seeds, 5 ice cubes

UK: 1 handful spinach, 1 medium apple (cored and chopped), 240ml water, 30g vanilla protein powder, 1 tablespoon flax seeds, 5 ice cubes

Instructions:

Add spinach, apple, water, vanilla protein powder, flax seeds, and ice cubes to your Nutribullet.

Secure the lid and blend on the Extract setting until well combined.

Pour into a glass and enjoy your nutritious green protein smoothie!

Nutritional Info: Calories: 180 Fat: 4g Carbs: 25g Protein: 18g

PEANUT BUTTER CUP PROTEIN SHAKE

Prep: 5 mins Cook: 0 mins Serves: 1 smoothie

Blending function used: Extract

Ingredients:

US: 240ml milk (or plantbased milk), 30g chocolate protein powder, 2 tablespoons peanut butter, 1 teaspoon vanilla extract, 5 ice cubes

UK: 240ml milk (or plantbased milk), 30g chocolate protein powder, 2 tablespoons peanut butter, 1 teaspoon vanilla extract, 5 ice cubes

Instructions:

Place milk, chocolate protein powder, peanut butter, vanilla extract, and ice cubes into your Nutribullet.

Secure the lid and blend on the Extract setting until smooth and creamy.

Pour into a glass and indulge in your delicious protein shake!

Nutritional Info: Calories: 350 Fat: 18g Carbs: 22g Protein: 25g

TROPICAL COCONUT PROTEIN SMOOTHIE

Prep: 5 mins Cook: 0 mins Serves: 1 smoothie

Blending function used: Extract

Ingredients:

US: 150g pineapple chunks (frozen), 240ml coconut milk, 30g vanilla protein powder, 1 tablespoon shredded coconut, 5 ice cubes

UK: 150g pineapple chunks (frozen), 240ml coconut milk, 30g vanilla protein powder, 1 tablespoon shredded coconut, 5 ice cubes

Instructions:

Combine pineapple chunks, coconut milk, vanilla protein powder, shredded coconut, and ice cubes in your Nutribullet.

Secure the lid and blend on the Extract setting until smooth.

Pour into a glass and enjoy your tropical protein smoothie!

Nutritional Info: Calories: 280 Fat: 12g Carbs: 30g Protein: 20g

CINNAMON ROLL PROTEIN BLAST

Prep: 5 mins Cook: 0 mins Serves: 1 smoothie

Blending function used: Extract

Ingredients:

US: 240ml milk (or plantbased milk), 30g vanilla protein powder, 1 teaspoon cinnamon, 1 tablespoon almond butter, 1 teaspoon maple syrup, 5 ice cubes

UK: 240ml milk (or plantbased milk), 30g vanilla protein powder, 1 teaspoon cinnamon, 1 tablespoon almond butter, 1 teaspoon maple syrup, 5 ice cubes

Instructions:

Add milk, vanilla protein powder, cinnamon, almond butter, maple syrup, and ice cubes to your Nutribullet.

Secure the lid and blend on the Extract setting until well mixed.

Pour into a glass and savour the flavours of a cinnamon roll in your protein smoothie!

Nutritional Info: Calories: 310 Fat: 14g Carbs: 28g Protein: 22g

COFFEE PROTEIN WAKEUP CALL

Prep: 5 mins Cook: 0 mins Serves: 1 smoothie

Blending function used: Extract

Ingredients:

US: 240ml cold brew coffee, 30g chocolate or vanilla protein powder, 1 tablespoon coconut oil, 1 teaspoon honey, 5 ice cubes

UK: 240ml cold brew coffee, 30g chocolate or vanilla protein powder, 1 tablespoon coconut oil, 1 teaspoon honey, 5 ice cubes

Instructions:

Combine cold brew coffee, protein powder, coconut oil, honey, and ice cubes in your Nutribullet.

Secure the lid and blend on the Extract setting until frothy and smooth.

Pour into a glass and kickstart your day with a caffeinated protein boost!

Nutritional Info: Calories: 240 Fat: 12g Carbs: 12g Protein: 20g

CHERRY VANILLA MUSCLE MENDER

Prep: 5 mins Cook: 0 mins Serves: 1 smoothie

Blending function used: Extract

Ingredients:

US: 150g cherries (frozen, pitted), 240ml almond milk, 30g vanilla protein powder, 1 tablespoon chia seeds, 5 ice cubes

UK: 150g cherries (frozen, pitted), 240ml almond milk, 30g vanilla protein powder, 1 tablespoon chia seeds, 5 ice cubes

Instructions:

Place cherries, almond milk, vanilla protein powder, chia seeds, and ice cubes into your Nutribullet. Secure the lid and blend on the Extract setting until smooth.

Pour into a glass and enjoy the sweet and tart flavours of your musclerepairing smoothie!

Nutritional Info: Calories: 210 Fat: 6g Carbs: 30g Protein: 15g

BLUEBERRY MUFFIN PROTEIN SHAKE

Prep: 5 mins Cook: 0 mins Serves: 1 smoothie

Blending function used: Extract

Ingredients:

US: 150g blueberries (frozen), 240ml milk (or plantbased milk), 30g vanilla protein powder, 1 tablespoon oats, 1 teaspoon honey, 5 ice cubes

UK: 150g blueberries (frozen), 240ml milk (or plantbased milk), 30g vanilla protein powder, 1 tablespoon oats, 1 teaspoon honey, 5 ice cubes

Instructions:

Add blueberries, milk, vanilla protein powder, oats, honey, and ice cubes to your Nutribullet. Secure the lid and blend on the Extract setting until smooth and creamy.

Pour into a glass and enjoy the taste of a blueberry muffin in your protein shake!

Nutritional Info: Calories: 250 Fat: 6g Carbs: 35g Protein: 18g

KEY LIME PIE PROTEIN SMOOTHIE

Prep: 5 mins | Cook: 0 mins | Serves: 1 smoothie

Blending function used: Extract

Ingredients:

US: 1 lime (juiced), 240ml coconut milk, 30g vanilla protein powder, 1 tablespoon Greek yoghurt, 1 teaspoon honey, 5 ice cubes

UK: 1 lime (juiced), 240ml coconut milk, 30g vanilla protein powder, 1 tablespoon Greek yoghurt, 1 teaspoon honey, 5 ice cubes

Instructions:

Combine lime juice, coconut milk, vanilla protein powder, Greek yoghurt, honey, and ice cubes in your Nutribullet.

Secure the lid and blend on the Extract setting until smooth.

Pour into a glass and enjoy your tangy, protein-packed smoothie!

Nutritional Info: Calories: 220 Fat: 10g Carbs: 20g Protein: 20g

CARROT CAKE PROTEIN SHAKE

Prep: 5 mins Cook: 0 mins Serves: 1 smoothie

Blending function used: Extract

Ingredients:

US: 1 medium carrot (grated), 240ml milk (or plant-based milk), 30g vanilla protein powder, 1 tablespoon Greek yoghurt, 1 teaspoon cinnamon, 1 teaspoon honey, 5 ice cubes

UK: 1 medium carrot (grated), 240ml milk (or plant-based milk), 30g vanilla protein powder, 1 tablespoon Greek yoghurt, 1 teaspoon cinnamon, 1 teaspoon honey, 5 ice cubes

Instructions:

Add grated carrot, milk, vanilla protein powder, Greek yoghurt, cinnamon, honey, and ice cubes to your Nutribullet.

Secure the lid and blend on the Extract setting until smooth and creamy.

Pour into a glass and indulge in the flavours of a carrot cake in your protein shake!

Nutritional Info: Calories: 240 Fat: 7g Carbs: 28g Protein: 20g

STRAWBERRY CHEESECAKE PROTEIN BLAST

Prep: 5 mins | Cook: 0 mins | Serves: 1 smoothie

Blending function used: Extract

Ingredients:

US: 150g strawberries (frozen), 240ml milk (or plant-based milk), 30g vanilla protein powder, 1 tablespoon cream cheese, 1 teaspoon honey, 5 ice cubes

UK: 150g strawberries (frozen), 240ml milk (or plant-based milk), 30g vanilla protein powder, 1 tablespoon cream cheese, 1 teaspoon honey, 5 ice cubes

Instructions:

Place strawberries, milk, vanilla protein powder, cream cheese, honey, and ice cubes into your Nutribullet.

Secure the lid and blend on the Extract setting until smooth and creamy.

Pour into a glass and enjoy the rich, indulgent taste of a strawberry cheesecake in your protein smoothie!

Nutritional Info: Calories: 260 Fat: 9g Carbs: 28g Protein: 20g

MEAL PLANNING WITH YOUR NUTRIBULLET

CREATING BALANCED MEAL PLANS

When I first started using my Nutribullet, I quickly realised its potential for revolutionising my meal planning. Creating balanced meal plans with your Nutribullet is not only easy but can also be quite fun. Let me share with you how I approach this to ensure I'm getting a good mix of nutrients throughout the week.

UNDERSTANDING BALANCED NUTRITION

Before we dive into meal planning, it's crucial to understand what constitutes a balanced diet. Generally, we're aiming for a mix of:

Carbohydrates for energy
Proteins for muscle repair and growth
Healthy fats for nutrient absorption and brain health
Vitamins and minerals for various bodily functions
Fibre for digestive health

With your Nutribullet, it's easy to incorporate all of these into your daily routine.

PLANNING YOUR WEEK

I find it helpful to plan my Nutribullet meals for the entire week. Here's a 4week Nutribullet meal plan Feel free to adjust portions or ingredients based on your preferences and nutritional needs.

WEEK 1

DAYS	BREAKFAST	LUNCH	DINNER
MONDAY	Glowing Green Goddess	Berry Collagen Booster	Cucumber Mint Refresher
TUESDAY	Carrot Ginger Glow	Avocado Spinach Hydrator	Pomegranate Antioxidant Blast
WEDNESDAY	Kiwi Vitamin C Kick	Papaya Enzyme Elixir	Aloe Vera Skin Soother
THURSDAY	Beetroot Beauty Blend	Mango Turmeric Radiance	Blueberry Acai Skin Shield
FRIDAY	Coconut Water Complexion Clearer	Berry AgeDefying Blend	Green Tea Antioxidant Smoothie
SATURDAY	Cacao Nib Youth Booster	Omega3 Rich Flaxseed Shake	Spirulina Superfood Elixir
SUNDAY (Special Occasion)	Pomegranate Seed Rejuvenator	Kale and Almond AntiWrinkle Blend	Goji Berry Longevity Tonic

WEEK 2

DAYS	BREAKFAST	LUNCH	DINNER
MONDAY	Avocado EBooster Smoothie	CollagenSupporting Citrus Blend	Resveratrolrich red Grape Smoothie
TUESDAY	Matcha Green Tea Energy Lift	Açai Berry AgeReversal Blend	Green Detox Dream
WEDNESDAY	Lemon Ginger Flush	Activated Charcoal Cleanse	Beet and Berry Liver Support
THURSDAY	Cilantro Chelation Blend	Dandelion Greens Detoxifier	Watermelon Flush
FRIDAY	Pineapple Enzyme Cleanser	Chlorella ClearOut	Cranberry Kidney Cleanse
SATURDAY	Apple Cider Vinegar Detox	Turmeric Golden Milk Detoxifier	Parsley and Celery Juice Blend
SUNDAY (Special Occasion)	Green Metabolism Booster	Berry Protein Punch	Cinnamon Roll Protein Shake

WEEK 3

DAYS	BREAKFAST	LUNCH	DINNER
MONDAY	Spinach and Pear Slimmer	Chia Seed Filling Smoothie	Grapefruit Fat Burner
TUESDAY	Chocolate PB2 Protein Shake	Cayenne KickStart Blend	Matcha Green Tea Fat Burner
WEDNESDAY	Celery and Apple Flat Belly Smoother	Pineapple Coconut Metabolism Booster	Raspberry Ketone Kicker
THURSDAY	Cucumber Mint Hydration Helper	Oatmeal Berry Heart Helper	Spinach Avocado Cholesterol Buster
FRIDAY	Beet and Pomegranate Pressure Reducer	Omega3 Rich Flax and Chia Blend	Green Tea and Berries Artery Cleaner
SATURDAY	Banana Walnut Potassium Booster	Kale and Pineapple Inflammation Fighter	Cocoa and Almond Heart Protector
SUNDAY (Special Occasion)	Tomato Lycopene Heart Shield	Watermelon Citrulline Cardio Booster	Grape and Resveratrol Heart Tonic

WEEK 4

DAYS	BREAKFAST	LUNCH	DINNER
MONDAY	Ginger Turmeric Circulation Enhancer	Blueberry Oat Fiber Booster	Espresso Protein Punch
TUESDAY	Green Tea Energiser	Beetroot PreWorkout Booster	Banana Oat Energy Blast
WEDNESDAY	Maca Root PowerUp	Ginseng Ginger Zing	Coconut Water Electrolyte Replenisher
THURSDAY	Cacao Nib Energy Bites Smoothie	Spirulina Superfood Energiser	Matcha Green Tea Focuser
FRIDAY	Chia Seed Sustainer	B Vitamin Boost Blend	Guarana Berry Energy Kick
SATURDAY	Acai Berry Bowl Blend	Goji Berry Antioxidant Blast	Spirulina Green Goddess
SUNDAY (Special Occasion)	Maca Root Hormone Balancer	Cacao Nib Mood Lifter	Chia Seed Omega Booster

TIPS FOR BALANCED MEAL PLANNING

Colour Variety: Aim for a rainbow of colours in your smoothies and sauces. Different colours often indicate different nutrients.

Protein Sources: Rotate between plant-based proteins (like nuts, seeds, and legumes) and animal proteins if you eat them.

Healthy Fats: Include sources of healthy fats daily, such as avocados, nuts, seeds, or olive oil.

Fibre Focus: Add vegetables to your smoothies and soups for added fibre.

Portion Control: Use your Nutribullet cups as a natural portion guide.

Hydration: Remember that smoothies can contribute to your daily fluid intake.

Seasonal Eating: Base your meal plans around seasonal produce for maximum nutrition and flavour.

Prep Ahead: Use your Sunday to prepare bases for smoothies or soups for the week ahead.

Remember, this is just a guide. Feel free to adjust based on your personal preferences and dietary needs. The beauty of the Nutribullet is its versatility – you can easily tweak recipes to suit your tastes and nutritional requirements.

By planning your meals and using your Nutribullet creatively, you'll find it's easy to maintain a balanced, nutritious diet without sacrificing flavour or spending hours in the kitchen. Happy planning and blending!

MEASUREMENT CONVERSIONS

As a UK-based Nutribullet enthusiast, I know how crucial accurate measurements are for perfect blends. Here's a handy conversion chart to help you navigate between metric and imperial measurements:

Metric	Imperial
15 ml	1 tablespoon
5 ml	1 teaspoon
30 ml	1 fl oz
60 ml	1/4 cup
80 ml	1/3 cup
120 ml	1/2 cup
240 ml	1 cup
250 ml	1 cup (liquid)
500 ml	2 cups / 1 pint
1 litre	4 cups / 2 pints
28 g	1 oz
454 g	1 lb

Remember, for most Nutribullet recipes, precise measurements aren't always necessary. Feel free to adjust to your taste!

Nutritional Information for All Recipes

Providing accurate nutritional information for each recipe ensures you can make informed choices about your diet. Here's a sample of how the nutritional information is presented for each recipe in this book:

GREEN DETOX DREAM (SERVES 1)		
Nutrient	Amount	% Daily Value
Calories	150	
Saturated Fat	0g	0%
Cholesterol	0mg	0%
Sodium	30mg	1%
Total Carbohydrate	30g	11%
Dietary Fibre	6g	21%
Sugars	20g	
Protein	5g	
Vitamin A		80%
Vitamin C		100%
Calcium		8%
Iron		10%

Per cent, Daily Values are based on a 2,000-calorie diet. Your daily values may be higher or lower depending on your calorie needs.

Note: The nutritional information provided is an estimate and can vary based on specific brands of ingredients used.

INDEX

A
Açai Berry AgeReversal Blend, 27
Activated Charcoal Cleanse, 29
Almond
  AntiWrinkle Blend (with Kale), 25
  Heart Protector (with Cocoa), 43
  Muscle Builder (Vanilla), 72
AntiAging Elixirs, 22 27
Apple
  Cider Vinegar Detox, 32
  Flat Belly Smoother (with Celery), 38
  Pie Smoothie, 62
  Pie A La Mode Smoothie, 69
Asparagus and Pea Spring Cleanse, 63
Autumn
  Fig and Honey Blend, 65
  Pumpkin Spice Smoothie, 60

B
Banana
  Energy Blast (with Oat), 48
  Nutella Shake, 71
  Protein Shake (Chocolate), 72
  Split Smoothie, 66
  Walnut Potassium Booster, 42
Bee Pollen Immunity Booster, 59
Beet(root)
  and Berry Liver Support, 29
  and Pomegranate Pressure Reducer, 41
  Beauty Blend, 20
  PreWorkout Booster, 47
Berry
  AgeDefying Blend, 22
  Antioxidant Blast (Goji), 54
  Blast Recovery Smoothie, 73
  Collagen Booster, 16
  Heart Helper (with Oatmeal), 40
  Hidden Veggie Blast, 66
  Protein Punch, 34
  Summer Blast, 60
Blueberry
  Acai Skin Shield, 21
  Muffin Protein Shake, 76
  Oat Fiber Booster, 46

C
Cacao Nib
  Energy Bites Smoothie, 50
  Mood Lifter, 56
  Youth Booster, 23
Carrot
  Cake Protein Shake, 77
  Ginger Glow, 17
Cayenne KickStart Blend, 37
Celery
  and Apple Flat Belly Smoother, 38
  Juice Blend (with Parsley), 33
Chia Seed
  Filling Smoothie, 36
  Omega Booster, 56

Rich Blend (with Flax), 41
Chlorella ClearOut, 31
Chocolate
  Banana Protein Shake, 72
  Chip Cookie Dough Shake, 67
  PB2 Protein Shake, 37
Cilantro Chelation Blend, 29
Cinnamon
  Persimmon Fall Warmer, 64
  Roll Protein Shake, 35
  Roll Protein Blast, 75
Citrus
  CollagenSupporting Blend, 26
  Winter Immune Booster, 61
Cocoa and Almond Heart Protector, 43
Coconut
  Pineapple Smoothie (Tropical), 70
  Protein Smoothie (Tropical), 74
  Water Complexion Clearer, 21
  Water Electrolyte Replenisher, 49
Coffee Protein WakeUp Call, 75
Common Issues and Solutions, 14
Conclusion, 91
Cranberry
  Kidney Cleanse, 32
  Orange Winter Tonic, 62
Creamsicle Dream, 68
Cucumber Mint
  Hydration Helper, 39
  Refresher, 17

D
Dandelion Greens Detoxifier, 30
Detox and Cleanse Smoothies, 2833

E
Energy Boosters, 4653
Espresso Protein Punch, 46

F
Fig and Honey Autumn Blend, 65
Flax(seed)
  and Chia Blend (Omega3 Rich), 41
  Shake (Omega3 Rich), 23

G
Ginger
  Carrot Glow, 17
  Lemon Flush, 28
  Turmeric Circulation Enhancer, 45
  Zing (with Ginseng), 49
Gingerbread Cookie Protein Shake, 64
Ginseng Ginger Zing, 49
Goji Berry
  Antioxidant Blast, 54
  Longevity Tonic, 25
Grape and Resveratrol Heart Tonic, 44
Grapefruit Fat Burner, 36
Green
  Detox Dream, 28
  Monster Shake, 67
  Protein Machine, 73
  Tea Antioxidant Smoothie, 22
  Tea and Berries Artery Cleaner, 42
  Tea Energiser, 47
  Tea Fat Burner (Matcha), 38
Guarana Berry Energy Kick, 53

H
Heart Health Heroes, 4046
Hemp Protein PowerUp, 56

I
Introduction, 7

K

Kale
  and Almond AntiWrinkle Blend, 25
  and Pineapple Inflammation Fighter, 43
Key Lime Pie Protein Smoothie, 77
KidFriendly Smoothies, 6671
Kiwi Vitamin C Kick, 18

L

Lemon Ginger Flush, 28

M

Maca Root
  Hormone Balancer, 55
  PowerUp, 48
Mango Turmeric Radiance, 20
Matcha Green Tea
  Antioxidant Elixir, 58
  Energy Lift, 27
  Fat Burner, 38
  Focuser, 51
Meal Planning with Your Nutribullet, 79
Measurement Conversions, 84
Moringa Leaf NutrientPacked Smoothie, 57
My Nutribullet Journey, 7

N

Nutella Banana Shake, 71

O

Oatmeal Berry Heart Helper, 40
Omega3 Rich
  Flax and Chia Blend, 41
  Flaxseed Shake, 23

P

Papaya Enzyme Elixir, 19
Parsley and Celery Juice Blend, 33
Peanut Butter
  and Jelly Smoothie, 67
  Cup Protein Shake, 74
Pineapple
  Coconut Metabolism Booster, 38
  Enzyme Cleanser, 31
Pomegranate
  Antioxidant Blast, 18
  Pressure Reducer (with Beet), 41
  Seed Rejuvenator, 24
PostWorkout Smoothies (ProteinPacked), 7278
ProteinPacked PostWorkout Smoothies, 7278
Purple Power Smoothie, 70

R

Radiant Skin Smoothies, 1621
Rainbow Fruit Smoothie, 68
Raspberry Ketone Kicker, 39

S

Seasonal Smoothie Specialties, 6065
Spinach
  and Pear Slimmer, 35
  Avocado
    Cholesterol Buster, 40
    Hydrator, 18
Spirulina
  Green Goddess, 55
  Superfood
    Elixir, 24
    Energiser, 50
Spring
  Greens Renewal Blend, 61
  Tonic (Strawberry Rhubarb), 65
Strawberry
  Cheesecake Protein Blast, 78

Milk, 69
Rhubarb Spring Tonic, 65
Superfood Sensations, 54–59
Summer Berry Blast, 60

T

Tomato Lycopene Heart Shield, 43
Tropical Coconut
 Pineapple Smoothie, 70
 Protein Smoothie, 74
Turmeric
 Golden Milk
  Blend, 57
  Detoxifier, 32
 Mango Radiance, 20

U

Understanding Your Nutribullet, 10

V

Vanilla Almond Muscle Builder, 72

W

Watermelon
 Citrulline Cardio Booster, 44
 Cooler, 61
 Flush, 30
 Slushie, 69
Weight Loss Wonders, 34–39
Wheatgrass Shot Smoother, 58
Winter Citrus Immune Booster, 61

CONCLUSION

As we reach the end of this Nutribullet journey, I hope you're feeling inspired and empowered to create your own nutritious and delicious blends. Remember, the recipes in this book are just the beginning - feel free to experiment and make them your own!

Throughout this book, we've explored the basics of using your Nutribullet, delved into the nutritional benefits of various ingredients, and discovered a world of flavours through our diverse recipe collection. From radiant skin smoothies to heart-healthy blends, and from energising elixirs to indulgent yet nutritious treats, your Nutribullet is truly a gateway to better health and exciting culinary experiences.

As you embark on your Nutribullet adventure, keep these key points in mind:

Listen to your body and adjust recipes to suit your tastes and nutritional needs.
Don't be afraid to experiment with new ingredients and combinations.
Make blending a part of your daily routine for consistent health benefits.
Keep your Nutribullet clean and well-maintained for optimal performance.
Share your creations with friends and family - spreading health and happiness is always rewarding!

Remember, health is a journey, not a destination. Your Nutribullet is a powerful tool on this journey, helping you to nourish your body with whole foods and plant-based nutrition easily and deliciously.

Thank you for joining me on this Nutribullet adventure. Here's to your health, happiness, and many satisfying blends to come!

HAPPY BLENDING!

Printed in Great Britain
by Amazon